T
Pocket Guide
to English
Architecture

The Pocket Guide to English Architecture

Philip Wilkinson

First published in Great Britain in 2009 by
REMEMBER WHEN
An imprint of
Pen & Sword Books Ltd
47 Church Street
Barnsley
South Yorkshire
S70 2AS

ISBN 978 1 84468 045 0

A CIP catalogue record for this book is available from the British Library

Printed and bound by CPI UK
Picture research by Fiona Shoop

Pen & Sword Books Ltd incorporates the Imprints of Pen & Sword Aviation, Pen & Sword Maritime, Pen & Sword Military, Wharncliffe Local History, Pen & Sword Select, Pen & Sword Military Classics, Leo Cooper, Remember When, Seaforth Publishing and Frontline Publishing

For a complete list of Pen & Sword titles please contact
PEN & SWORD BOOKS LIMITED
47 Church Street, Barnsley, South Yorkshire, S70 2AS, England
E-mail: enquiries@pen-and-sword.co.uk
Website: www.pen-and-sword.co.uk

Contents

Timeline

c. 600–1066 Saxon

c. 680	Brixworth Church, Northamptonshire
c. 680	Escomb Church, County Durham
700s	Bradford-on-Avon Church, Wiltshire
c 760–870	Crypt of Repton church, Derbyshire
c. 990	Tower of Barton on Humber church, Lincolnshire

1066–c. 1200 Norman

c. 1086–97	White Tower, Tower of London
1093–1132	Durham Cathedral (p16)
1096–1145	Norwich Cathedral (p17)
1117–93	Peterborough Cathedral
1126–39	Keep of Rochester Castle, Kent
1135	onwards Fountains Abbey, Yorkshire
1166–72	Keep of Orford Castle, Suffolk
1174–85	Choir of Canterbury Cathedral
c. 1180	'Jew's House', Lincoln
c. 1190	Manor House, Boothby Pagnell, Lincolnshire

St Albans Abbey

c. 1200–c.1300 Early English Gothic

c. 1180–1425	Wells Cathedral (p31)
1192–1235	Lincoln Cathedral
c 1193–1230	West front of Peterborough Cathedral
1220–58	Salisbury Cathedral (p23)
c. 1220	Choir of Beverley Minster, Yorkshire
1225–40	Nave of Rievaulx Abbey, Yorkshire
1233	West front of Ripon Cathedral
1245–69	Eastern parts of Westminster Abbey

York Minster

c. 1300–c.1350 Decorated Gothic

c. 1300–c. 1350	Heckington Church, Lincolnshire
c. 1300–c. 1350	Patrington Church, Yorkshire
1306–32	Choir of Bristol Cathedral
1320–40	East end of Wells Cathedral
1322–40	Octagonal lantern of Ely Cathedral
1327–69	Vaulting of Exeter Cathedral

The curvilinear window typical of the style, as seen at Beverley Minster

c. 1337–c. 1540 Perpendicular Gothic

c. 1337–1360	Choir of Gloucester Cathedral (p45)
1351–64	Cloister of Gloucester Cathedral (p47)
1380–1420	West front of Beverley Minster, Yorkshire
c. 1425	Choir of Sherborne Abbey
1446–1515	King's College Chapel, Cambridge (p44)
1475–1511	St George's Chapel, Windsor Castle
1490–1503	Central tower of Canterbury Cathedral
1501–39	Bath Abbey
1503–9	Henry VII's Chapel, Westminster Abbey

King's College, Cambridge

c. 1500–c. 1600 Tudor

1562–70	Middle Temple Hall, London
1567–80	Longleat House, Wiltshire (p55)
1570–75	Kirby Hall, Northamptonshire
1577–87	Burghley House, Leicestershire
1580–88	Wollaton Hall, Nottinghamshire
1580–99	Montacute House, Somerset

Hampton Court Palace

c. 1600–c. 1660 Palladian

1619–22 Banqueting House, Whitehall, London (p58)
1616–35 Queen's House, Greenwich, London (p57)
1631–35 St Paul's Church, Covent Garden, London (p59)
1632–49 Wilton House, Wiltshire

Royal Hospital, Greenwich

c. 1660–c. 1720 English baroque

1671–8, 1701–3	St Bride's, Fleet Street, London
1672–79	St Stephen's, Walbrook, London
1675–1710	St Paul's Cathedral, London (p63)
1677–80	Town Hall, Abingdon, Oxfordshire
1683	Custom House, King's Lynn, Norfolk
1689–94	Fountain Court etc, Hampton Court Palace, London
1696–1715	Greenwich Hospital, London (p68–9)
1699–1712	Castle Howard, Yorkshire
1704–20	Blenheim Palace, Oxfordshire (p66)

Tom Tower Christ Church, Oxford

c. 1715–c. 1760 Palladian Revival

c. 1722–25	Mereworth Castle, Kent (p80)
1722–26	Houghton Hall, Norfolk (p85)
1722–26	St Martin-in-the-Fields, London
1724–29	Chiswick House, London
1731–2	Assembly Rooms, York
1734–61	Holkham Hall, Norfolk
1745–58	Horse Guards, Whitehall, London (p78)

Horse Guards, Whitehall

c. 1760–c.1790 Neo-Classicism

1761–80	Interiors of Osterley Park, Middlesex
1762–69	Interiors of Syon House, Middlesex
1765–67	All Hallows on the Wall, London
1765–70	Interiors of Kedleston Hall, Derbyshire
1776–86	Somerset House, London

c. 1740–c. 1820 Gothick

1741–48	Gothic Temple, Stowe, Buckinghamshire
1747–63	Strawberry Hill, Twickenham, London
1750	Adlestrop Park, Gloucestershire
1753–55	Remodelling of Lacock Abbey, Wiltshire
1753	Shobdon Church, Herefordshire
1771–1776	Arbury Hall, Warwickshire
1777–81	Tetbury Church, Gloucestershire
1803–13	Ashridge Park, Hertfordshire

Eaton Hall

c. 1760–c. 1815 The Picturesque and the Exotic

1761	Pagoda, Royal Botanic Gardens, Kew
1803–15	Sezincote, Gloucestershire
1805	Cronkhill, Shropshire
1807–10	Caerhays Castle, Cornwall
1810–11	Blaise Hamlet, Bristol
1815–21	Royal Pavilion, Brighton, Sussex (p95)

Brighton Pavilion

c. 1770–c. 1850 The Industrial Revolution

1771	Arkwright's Mill, Cromford, Derbyshire
1796	Marshall, Benyon and Bage Mill, Ditherington, Shrewsbury
1797	East Mill, Belper, Derbyshire
1813	Stanley Mill, King's Stanley, Gloucestershire
1828–31	Middle Warehouse, Middle Basin, Castlefield, Manchester
1838–40	Temple Mill, Leeds
1840s	The Albert Dock, Liverpool

c. 1790–c. 1830 Classical Revivals

1772–94	Radcliffe Observatory, Oxford
1813–18	St Marylebone Church, London
1819–22	St Pancras Church, London
1823–47	The British Museum, London
c. 1827	Cumberland Terrace, Regent's Park, London
1827–28	University College, London
1833–38	National Gallery, London

Marble Arch, London

c. 1830–c. 1890 Gothic Revival

1836–68	Houses of Parliament, London (p103)
1841	St Giles's, Cheadle, Staffordshire
1849–59	All Saints, Margaret Street, London
1855–59	University Museum, Oxford (p104)
1865–71	St Pancras Hotel and Station, London
1867–83	Keble College, Oxford
1868–77	Manchester Town Hall
1871–82	Royal Courts of Justice, London
1879–1910	Truro Cathedral

University Museum, Oxford

c. 1836– c. 1865 Iron and Glass

1836–40	Conservatory, Chatsworth, Derbyshire
1845–47	Palm House, Royal Botanic Gardens, Kew
1850–52	King's Cross Station, London
1852–54	Paddington Station, London
1863–67	St Pancras Station, London, Train Shed (p113)
1864–65	Oriel Chambers, Liverpool

St Pancras Station

c. 1840–c. 1900 Victorian Variety

1840–54	St George's Hall, Liverpool
1853–54	Free Trade Hall, Manchester
1853–59	Leeds Town Hall
1866–67	Glen Andred, Groombridge, Sussex
1870	Cragside, Northumberland
1887–88	New Scotland Yard, London
1888	170, Queen's Gate, London
1895–1903	Westminster Cathedral

c. 1870–c. 1910 Arts and Crafts

1887	Wightwick Manor, Staffordshire
1898–99	Broadleys, Windermere, Cumbria
1898–99	Blackwell, Bowness, Cumbria
1900–01	Deanery Garden, Sonning, Berkshire
1901	The Pastures, North Luffenham, Rutland
1901–02	Brockhampton church, Herefordshire
1906–07	St Andrew's Church, Roker, Sunderland

c. 1870–c. 1920 Garden and Suburb

1870s and 1880s	Bedford Park, London
1901–	New Earswick, York
1903–	Letchworth, Hertfordshire
1905–	Hampstead Garden Suburb, London
1920–	Welwyn Garden City, Hertfordshire

c. 1890–c. 1914 The Turn of the Century

1897–99	Whitechapel Art Gallery, London
1898–1902	Town Hall, Colchester, Essex
1899–1902	Westminster College, Cambridge
1900	Royal Arcade, Norwich
1900–06	Old Bailey Criminal Courts, London
1902	Horniman Museum, Forest Hill, London
1904	Great Warley Church, Essex
1905–07	Bristol Central Library
1905–08	Piccadilly Hotel, London

c. 1920–1939 Modernism

1928–29	High and Over, Amersham, Buckinghamshire
1930	Arnos Grove Underground Station, London
1930	Royal Corinthian Yacht Club, Burnham-on-Crouch, Essex
1930–32	Boots Factory, Beeston, Nottinghamshire
1935	De la Warr Pavilion, Bexhill, Sussex
1938–39	Finsbury Health Centre, London

c. 1925–1939 Art Deco and Moderne

1920s	Great London House, Mornington Crescent, London
1932	Daily Express Building, Fleet Street, London
1932	Hays Wharf, London
1932–37	Hoover Building, Western Avenue, London
1934	RIBA Building, Portland Place, London
1939	Eltham Palace, London

Introduction

ARCHITECTURE is the one art form that affects us all. We spend our whole lives using buildings and looking at them. We pour more money into our houses than anything else, and we use much of our leisure time doing them up – or visiting castles, country houses, cathedrals, and museums. And, as we make our way from one to the other, buildings are around us, everywhere.

As John Betjeman once wrote, the buildings that surround us are like 'a public art gallery which is always open'. In fact, our built environment is like one of those old-fashioned art galleries, the ones that contained so many pictures, they had to be hung from floor to ceiling. It is easy to miss things in such a crowded setting. Go off the beaten track, down a side street in an English town for example, and you can discover fascinating old buildings neglected by the tourist guides. Look up above the shop fronts in a typical high street and you will find the façades of older shops and houses, tantalising evidence of former architectural glories.

As with any public art gallery, the collection has been built up slowly over the years. It includes buildings that are large and small, old and new, shocking and bland. Some we love and some leave us cold, and we are not always sure why they got to be they way they are – we do not know much about architecture, but we know what we like.

This book aims to inform our journeys from one building to the next, and to make them more enjoyable. It tells the story of the main architectural styles and ways of building in England, from the Saxon era to the Twentieth Century. It describes each style briefly, highlighting key features and mentioning major historical events such as the Norman Conquest and the Industrial Revolution, so that the developments in building appear in context. And it illustrates the story with some of the most outstanding examples. It is a concise book, because its subject is the *essence* of each period not the endless variations played by builders and architects on each basic theme. Each small section is like a window into a style or period, highlighting some of the best examples. Each has its own story, its own values, its own special delight. Open your eyes, look up, and enjoy . . .

The beginnings (before 1066)

PEOPLE have lived in Britain for thousands of years and must have built themselves shelters for much of this time. But the buildings of our prehistoric ancestors have long vanished and the main evidence of prehistoric structural skills can be found in monuments and stone circles such as Stonehenge – exceptional as structures, but not actually buildings. By the time the Romans arrived in Britain in AD 43, they invaded a land with quite sophisticated wooden buildings. Archaeologists have reconstructed the round houses of the ancient Britons but the originals, made of wood and thatch, have long perished. The Roman invaders, by contrast, built in brick and stone, and worked on a vast scale. But their towns, forts, temples, and villas now exist only as ruins. Much as they tell us about life in the Roman period and about Roman technology – especially the Romans' famous use of 'modern' materials like concrete and their sophisticated underfloor heating – they are fascinating fragments only.

The oldest English standing buildings date from the Anglo-Saxon period, the centuries between the departure of the Romans in the early Fifth Century and the Norman Conquest in 1066. In this period, people built mainly in wood, but some of the grander buildings, especially churches, were built in more durable stone. So, the few remaining stone buildings from this time are churches that date from the last centuries of the Saxon era, the period c. 600 to 1066. These are mostly quite simple buildings, with a few, small, round-headed windows, round- or triangular-

Saxon

Walls: High

Windows: Small; round- or triangular-headed

Doorways: Narrow, round-headed

Decorative details: Pilaster strips on walls; long-and-short quoins (cornerstones) headed doorways, and narrow arches. Most are quite plain but a few, like the church tower at Earls Barton, are adorned outside with narrow bands of slightly raised masonry, called pilaster strips, which make patterns that remind some historians of the framework of timber buildings.

Norman 1066 –c. 1200

AFTER the Norman Conquest, there was a building boom in England. The conquerors placed Norman lords in castles to control their new territory and soon Norman bishops and abbots were leading the church, too. Political domination went hand-in-hand with architectural domination, and some of the structures built by the incomers were larger than anything seen here before. The Normans' cathedrals and many of their castles were shockingly huge, and structures such as Durham Cathedral and the Tower of London must have inspired awe among the locals: the conquerors meant business, and it showed. What is more, most of these major buildings – and many of the lesser ones, especially Norman parish churches – were built of stone. They have survived in large numbers.

The Normans developed a massive building style to go with their image of power. It is an architecture of thick walls and narrow windows, massive columns and semi-circular arches. These arches are sometimes plain, sometimes moulded, and sometimes enriched with stylised carving in zigzag, cable, or other patterns. This decoration got more elaborate as time went on, and some late-Norman churches are a mass of dazzling

Norman

Walls: Thick, massive; very shallow buttresses

Ceilings: Barrel or tunnel vaults

Windows: Round-headed, sometimes with paired openings under one semi-circular arch; splayed openings

Doorways: Round-headed; often with several recessed arches or 'orders'

Arches: Semi-circular

Piers: Round, often fat, topped with cushion or scalloped capitals

Decorative details: Zig-zag, cable (rope), pellet, and other mouldings; beakhead carvings; blind arcading

zigzag and intricate blind arcading. Even small parish churches, such as Kilpeck, can be showcases of the carver's art.

Semi-circular arches and zigzag carved decoration mark the Norman porch at Southwell Minster. The building also boasts a fine Norman west front.

The lower stages of Durham Cathedral's twin west towers are Norman. Inside, the Norman nave, with its imposing piers, is a stunning space.

Rows of round arches supported on chunky piers line the Norman nave at Norwich Cathedral. The vaulted ceiling is later.

The choir of Durham Cathedral still retains its semi-circular Norman arches supported on round piers, one carved with a bold spiral motif.

Norman doorways often have recessed arches, called orders, The chevron or zigzag pattern was a favourite way of decorating these arches.

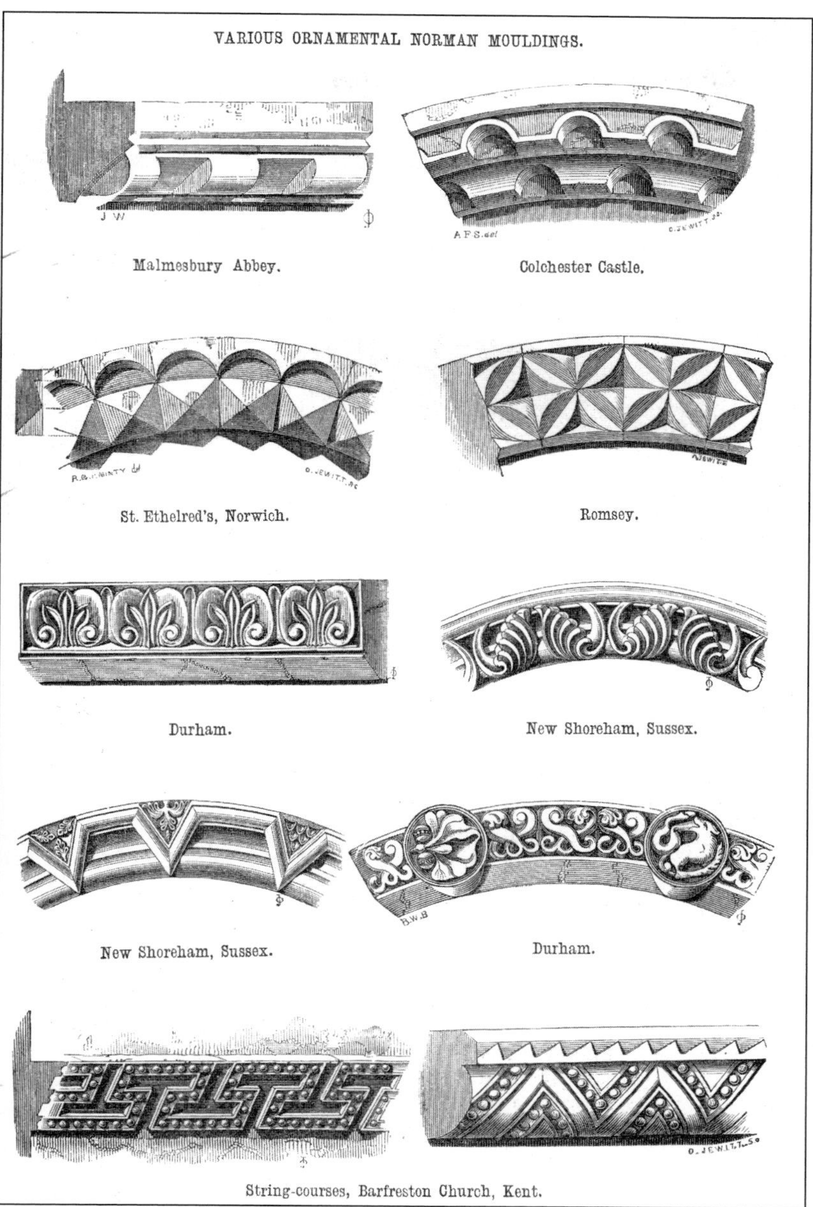

The Normans had a huge repertoire of ornaments, from the pyramidal nailhead, to the zigzag, which they used around arches and doorways.

Gothic c. 1200–c. 1500

GOTHIC architecture, developed in France, dominated English building after about 1200. This is the architecture of pointed arches, big windows, thinner walls, ribbed stone vaults and flying buttresses adopted by the cathedral- and church-builders.

Early English Gothic 1200–1300

Thirteenth-century Gothic in England – often known by its Victorian name of Early English – features narrow, pointed windows called lancets, which are sometimes grouped together to form composite windows. As the century progressed, these windows became more complex, with roundels and quatrefoils of glass added above the lancets to form simple tracery.

Interiors display deeply moulded arches and columns sometimes surrounded by clusters of slenderer columns known as shafts. The way in which the mouldings and shafts break up the surface of the stone of Early English arches and columns gives churches like Eaton Bray or cathe-

Early English Gothic c. 1200–1300

Roofs: Steeply pitched

Walls: Thinner than previously; often supported with buttresses; flying buttresses on larger churches

Ceilings: Ribbed vaults

Windows: Lancets (slender, pointed), often in groups of three or more; later simple tracery

Doorways: Pointed, with recessed orders and shafts

Arches: Pointed; often moulded

Piers: Round or other shapes often with detached shafts

Decorative details: 'Stiff-leaf' capitals

drals such as Wells a feeling of lightness, combined with a linear quality, quite different from the buildings of the Norman period. Many Early English churches are crowned with spires, emphasizing the way that the pointed arches and pinnacles of their Gothic architecture seem to point towards heaven.

Salisbury Cathedral's Lady Chapel features slender shafts, a delicate vault, and narrow lancet windows – all typical of the Early English style.

A forest of pinnacles and buttresses marks the exterior of Canterbury as a Gothic cathedral on the grand scale.

Salisbury is the only English cathedral built largely in one style, the Early English Gothic of the Thirteenth Century. The only exception is the slightly later spire.

Much of Lincoln Cathedral was built in the Thirteenth Century, the builders taking full advantage of a prominent hilltop site.

Richly moulded arches and geometrical window tracery made up of patterns of circles mark Lincoln's Thirteenth-century choir.

Behind the west front of Westminster Abbey is the imposing early Gothic church begun by Henry III in 1245. The twin west towers are an Eighteenth-century interpretation of Gothic.

Rows of lancets like these in the north transept of the great Gothic church of Beverley Minster were the preferred windows of the early-Thirteenth Century.

Polebrook church, Northamptonshire, has a broach spire with sloping, wedge-shaped supports at the corners, a favourite design of the Early English masons.

Lancet windows were often grouped in threes, the central one slightly taller than the other two, as at Polebrook.

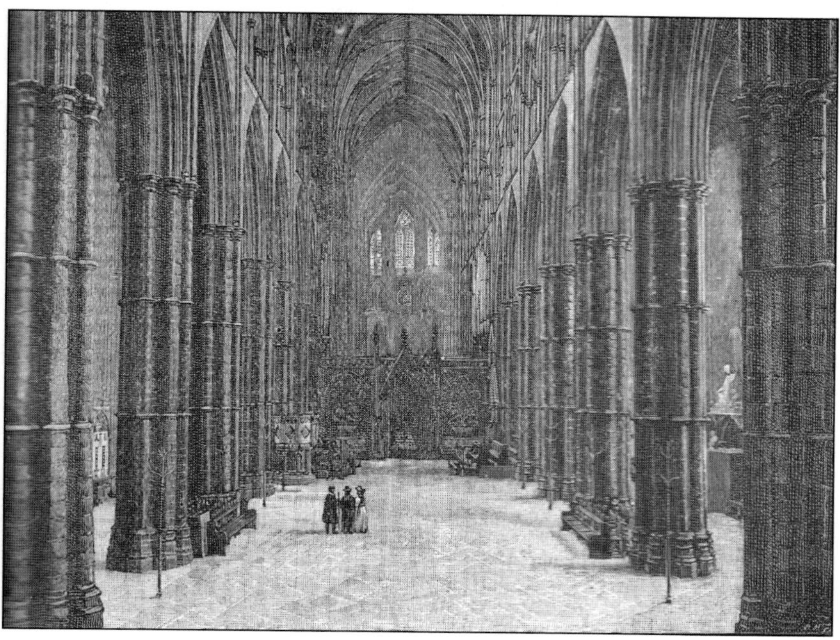

The nave of Westminster Abbey, with its tall clustered piers and narrow pointed arches, is one of the masterpieces of Early English architecture.

Lancet-shaped openings were sometimes decorated with rich carving. Stylised foliage was a favourite design, as here at Raunds church, Northamptonshire.

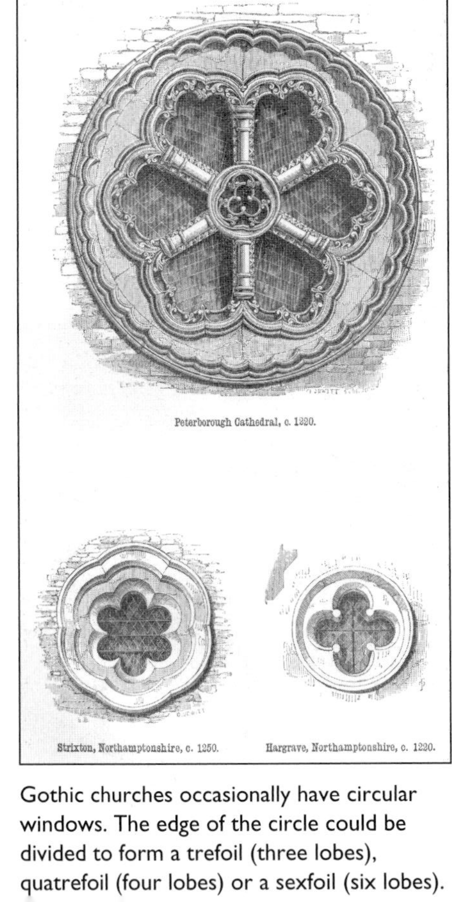

Gothic churches occasionally have circular windows. The edge of the circle could be divided to form a trefoil (three lobes), quatrefoil (four lobes) or a sexfoil (six lobes).

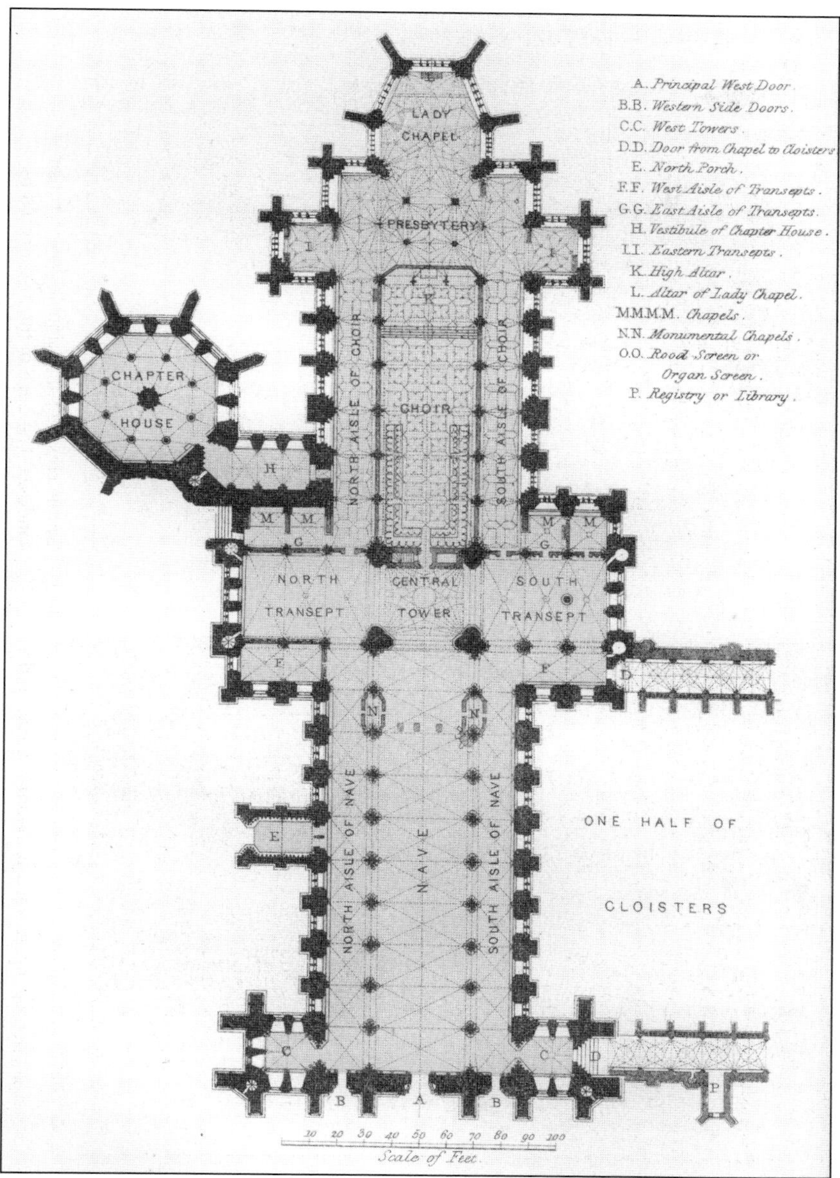

The Medieval cathedral-builders developed the cross-shaped plan. The choir was reserved for the clergy, the nave for the lay congregation, and the transepts and other spaces for extra chapels and altars.

Decorated Gothic 1300–1350

During the first half of the Fourteenth Century, Gothic architecture became more ornate. Complex, flowing tracery, florid carving, naturalistic foliage decoration, and a range of ornamental motifs earned the style its Victorian name, Decorated. It was still mainly an ecclesiastical style of architecture, perfectly suited to designing niches for statues of saints and slender crocketed spires, and exemplified in parish churches such as Heckington and Patrington. But a number of houses, such as the magnificent Penshurst Place, also survive with windows in the Decorated style, with features such as double-curved ogee arches and a huge variety of window tracery. English Decorated architecture branched out in exciting directions. But disaster stunted this burgeoning growth. The arrival of the Black Death in 1349 decimated the labour force and slowed building down, so most examples of the Decorated style date from the first half of the century.

Decorated Gothic c 1300–1350

Roofs: Pitched

Ceilings: Vaults with more intricate patterns of ribs

Windows: Broader; more complex tracery in geometrical or curvilinear patterns

Arches: Pointed; often intricately moulded; occasionally ogee (double-curve) shaped

Decorative details: More naturalistic foliate carving, ballflowers, pinnacles

The west front of York Minster has a vast window with the complex flowing tracery typical of the most sophisticated form of Decorated Gothic architecture. York's beautiful windows are unusual in England in that most of them still have their original Medieval stained glass.

With its rows of niches, trio of ornate spires, and complex window tracery, Lichfield Cathedral typifies Decorated Gothic.

At Howden church, Yorkshire, the elaborate pinnacles adorned with crockets are notable Decorated features.

The curvaceous tracery of this opening at St Mary's, Beverley, and the ogee arch below, are favourite motifs of the Fourteenth Century.

Finedon church, Northamptonshire, was built in the Fourteenth Century. The elegant spire is a typical feature of the churches of Northamptonshire.

This huge window at Hull shows the inventiveness of Gothic masons when designing tracery on a large scale.

Rose windows offered the mason great opportunities for tracery. This one at Cheltenham is one of a number of impressive Decorated windows in the church.

The Jesse window at Dorchester, Oxfordshire, is unique in that the tracery is carved with figures to form a Biblical family tree.

In the ruins of Tintern Abbey, on a stunning site overlooking the River Wye, some intricate window tracery has survived.

Perpendicular Gothic 1337–1540

At the same time that the Decorated style was being perfected, a completely new style was evolving in buildings such as Gloucester Cathedral, where the choir was remodelled in the 1330s to accommodate the tomb of King Edward II, who had recently been murdered in nearby Berkeley Castle. This new style, now known as Perpendicular, spread throughout the country during the Fifteenth Century. In some ways, the Fifteenth Century was a time of uncertainty. In the Wars of the Roses (1455–85) the Houses of Lancaster and York fought over the crown. But, for many, it was also a prosperous time, with English merchants earning fortunes in the wool trade. Their wealth and confidence is reflected in this Perpendicular phase of English Gothic. The name comes from the emphasis on verticals, such as window mullions and shafts, which can soar from the floor to the ceiling of a building. The other key feature is the virtual disappearance of the wall. In many Perpendicular buildings, the walls are 'dissolved' into screens of glass, and flying buttresses are used to hold up the roofs and ceilings. In the grandest structures, such as the choir of Gloucester Cathedral (p45) or King's College Chapel, Cambridge (p44), these ceilings are covered with intricate webs of vaulting, though many Perpendicular buildings – both churches and the great halls of big houses – have magnificent timber roofs that are masterpieces of carpentry. From the outside, these roofs are often virtually invisible, because they are shallow in pitch and concealed behind a parapet, pierced and carved to form a decorative feature in their own right. But inside, Perpendicular roofs can be extravaganzas of woodwork decorated with tracery and, sometimes, adorned with carvings of angels that seem about to take off in soaring flight from the beams and rafters (p131).

Perpendicular Gothic c 1337–1540

Roofs: Shallow pitched

Ceilings: Delicate fan vaults; wooden roofs decorated with carvings

Windows: Broad, with complex tracery; mullions (upright glazing bars) run all the way up the window

Doorways: Broad, sometimes with 'four-centred' (flattened pointed) opening

Arches: Pointed, moulded

Decorative details: Widespread use of 'panel' design to produce tracery-like effect of stone mouldings on walls, ceilings, and other surfaces

In the Lady Chapel of Gloucester Cathedral hundreds of vertical shafts and window mullions show why the Victorians called this style Perpendicular. The cathedral choir is in the same style on a still larger scale. (p45)

Oxford's Divinity School, now part of the Bodleian Library, shows how the late-Gothic builders liked to experiment with intricate patterns of vaulting ribs. Big windows flood the room with light.

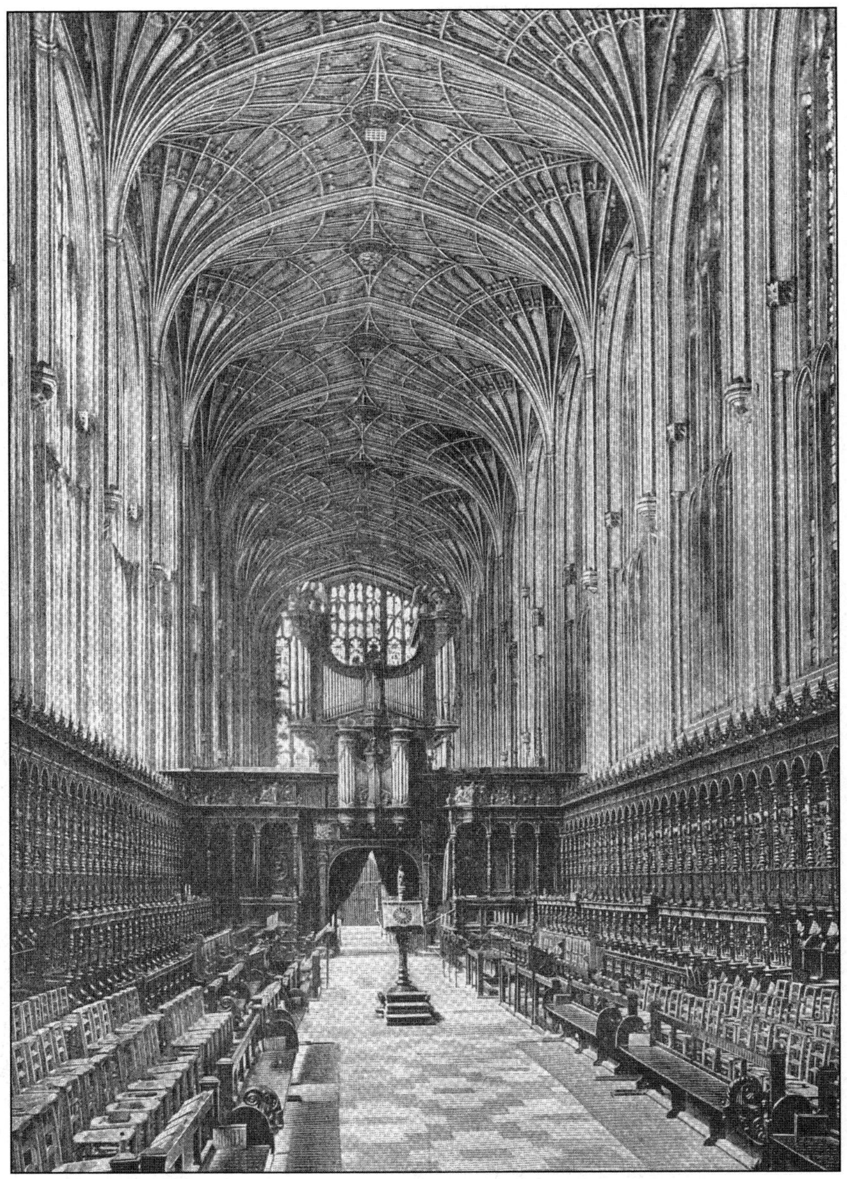

King's College Chapel, Cambridge, is one large room in the Perpendicular style. The vast windows stretch almost from floor to ceiling, and the fan vault is one of the finest anywhere.

The choir of Gloucester Cathedral is dominated by the enormous east window and the vertical shafts lining the walls on either side.

This chapel, part of a Perpendicular church at Evesham, Worcestershire, has a beautiful fan vault. The windows and entrance have flattened arches typical of the period.

The lovely church at Fotheringhay, Northamptonshire, was once much bigger. Large Perpendicular windows survive, together with a tower topped with an octagonal lantern made up almost completely of tracery.

Above, left: The central tower at Canterbury Cathedral, known as Bell Harry, was built right at the end of the Fifteenth Century. Its elegance is emphasised by the vertical lines that run all the way up the corner buttresses.

Above, right: The cloisters at Gloucester Cathedral have a beautiful fan vault covered with tracery and rows of Perpendicular windows.

Perpendicular tracery could cover walls as well as windows. This example, at St Michael's Coslaney, Norwich, is made up of a pattern of different coloured stones known as flushwork.

The tomb of Edward II is one of the highlights of Gloucester Cathedral. Its mass of pinnacles and openings is like a tiny building within the building.

Interlude: The Vernacular House

GOTHIC was the style for churches and grand houses and such buildings were the work of highly skilled master masons. Ordinary houses were a different matter. They were the work of local people, using basic skills and materials available nearby. In other words, they were vernacular architecture, a tradition of building that dates from earlier than the Middle Ages.

Vernacular houses vary in materials and appearance from one region to another. Where there is good building stone, cottages and farmhouses are built of this local material. The traditional houses of the limestone belt, for example, which runs from Somerset through Gloucestershire, parts of Oxfordshire, Northamptonshire, and northwards to parts of Lincolnshire and Yorkshire, are built of this beautiful and versatile material. Cornwall has cottages of granite, Cheshire houses of sandstone, Derbyshire buildings of millstone grit, all local stones. Flint is used for building in parts of Dorset and East Anglia. In other places, where building stone is rare, poor, or non-existent, timber-framed buildings are common, as in the West Midlands and Suffolk; or clay is used to make cob walls, as in Devon.

This rich variety of materials was exploited for centuries. If vernacular buildings differ greatly from region to region, they changed relatively little over time. So some cottages have Medieval origins, many date from the Tudor period, some are Georgian. And there are still builders working today, extending old cottages and building anew, using versions of the vernacular developed by their ancestors.

Tudor c. 1500–c. 1600

FEW CHURCHES were built during the Tudor period, especially after Henry VIII made his break with Rome in 1534, so the majority of surviving Tudor buildings are houses. Timber-framed structures were still common for houses, with many variations developed from the local vernacular styles. But, in places where stone was available, the Tudors built houses in a style that often looks like a domestic version of Perpendicular Gothic – there are big mullioned windows like the ones in churches, but they either have flattened arches or a completely rectangular shape.

Towards the end of the century, builders began to introduce Renaissance elements from continental Europe – for example, Classical pilasters from Italy and ornate, curvy gables from Holland. Features like these can be combined with very English-looking elements such as Tudor windows and strapwork, a form of low-relief linear decoration that looks rather like a pattern of leather straps that is common in English stonework and woodwork of the period. In the richer houses, carvers and plasterers added figures from mythology and folklore, such as mermaids and sea-dragons, developing the whole mixture into a striking hybrid style. This eclectic mix is visible in some of our most stunning country houses, such

Tudor

Walls: Dominated by big windows

Roofs: Flat or shallow-pitched

Ceilings: Moulded plaster or panelled wood

Windows: Large; rectangular or topped with four-centred arches; many lights with leaded panes; bay and oriel windows common

Doorways: Rectangular or four-centred

Decorative details: Strapwork, pilasters, niches, complex openwork parapets, turrets, 'linenfold' panelling; some use of Classical detailing, sometimes crudely interpreted; ornate chimneys as Wollaton Hall and Burghley House, with their towers, turrets, and amazing skylines.

By the beginning of the Seventeenth Century, this hybrid style was producing buildings that were strong both in overall shape and in fine detail. With bay windows, fancy openwork parapets, turrets glazed like observation platforms, and statues in niches, Elizabethan façades are some of the most interesting and eventful in the history of English architecture. The interiors are absorbing, too, with the development of exciting spaces such as long galleries or the elaboration of details like plaster ceilings and stone fire surrounds.

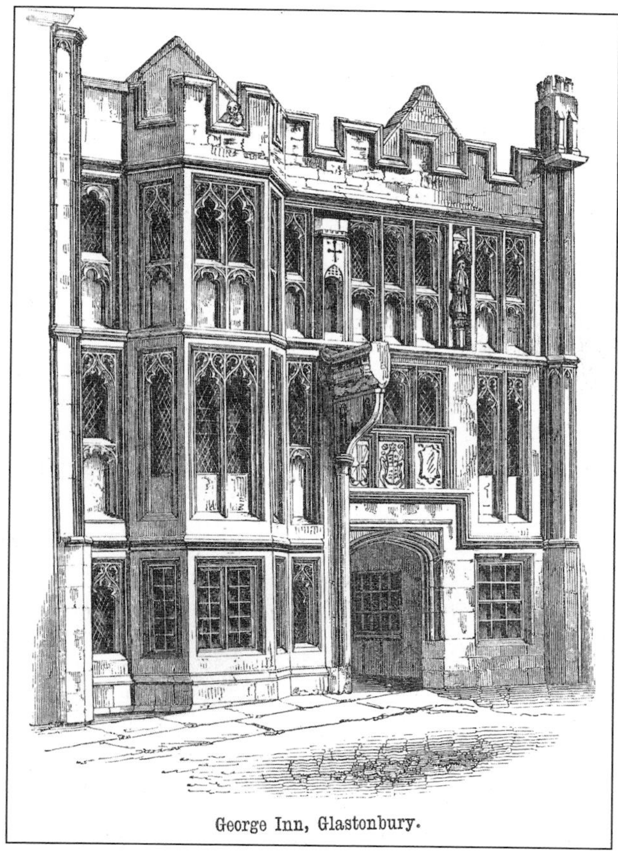

George Inn, Glastonbury.

The George Inn at Glastonbury, built in the early-Sixteenth Century, shows how Tudor builders used some Gothic features, but made them more domestic in style, rejecting pointed openings for square windows, for example.

A bold pattern of timbers above and an opening for the shopkeeper below – this house in Shrewsbury shows a common type of Tudor town house. Buildings like this have now been converted to modern glass-windowed shops.

Christ Church Hall, Oxford, A.D. 1528.

Tudor builders liked rich decoration. This example is from the interior of the hall at Christ Church, Oxford.

This row of arches at St James' Palace, London, shows the flattened or four-centred design favoured by many Tudor builders. Battlements were also a favourite motif, although they no longer had their Medieval defensive use.

Hampton Court Palace, London evolved over centuries, and is in several different styles. This early engraving shows some of the Tudor portions, including the hall to the left.

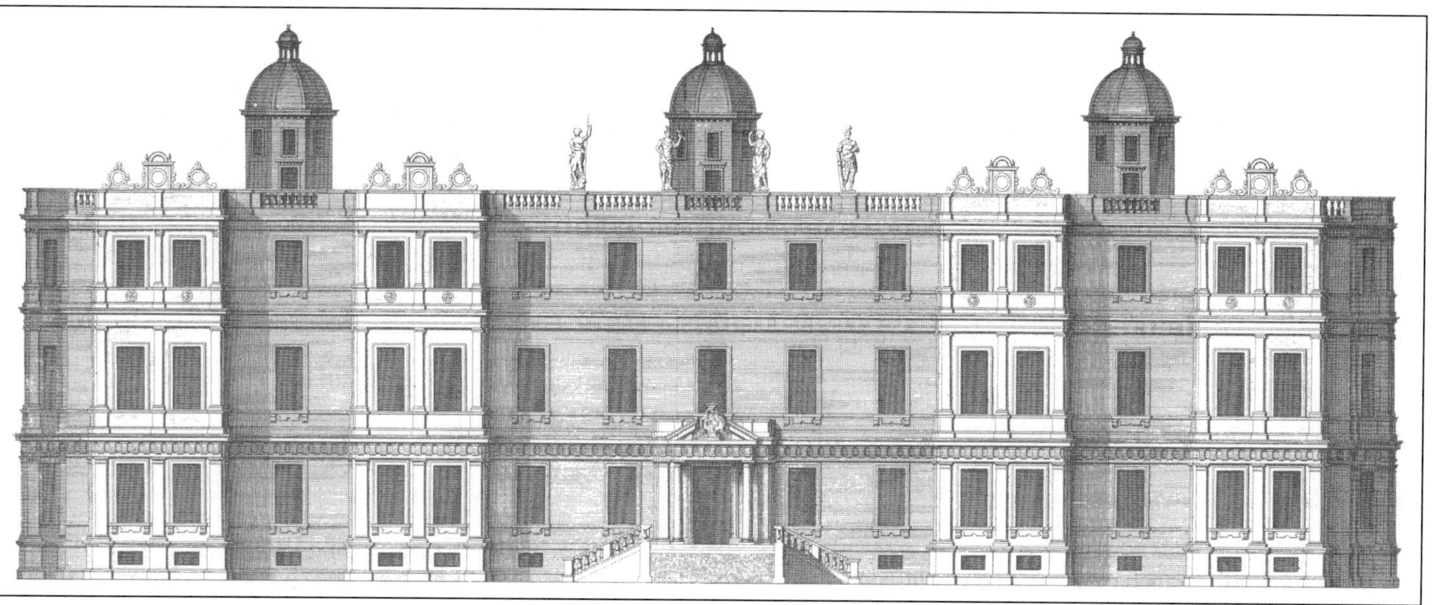

Longleat is one of the magnificent ‘Prodigy Houses’ of the Sixteenth Century. Its skyline is enlivened with statues and little domed ‘banqueting houses’.

Palladian c. 1600–c. 1660

IN THE early-Seventeenth Century, there was an earth-shattering change in English architecture. The architect and designer Inigo Jones discovered the writings of Palladio and the buildings of Italy. Andrea Palladio was an Italian architect whose *Quattro Libri dell'Architettura* (*Four Books of Architecture*) became the new textbook for builders. Palladio measured and drew the buildings of ancient Rome, publicised the work of the Roman architectural theorist Vitruvius, and designed numerous villas in the Classical style in northern Italy. Jones made two trips to Italy himself, and, on the second, he took a copy of Palladio with him, making notes as he went. Jones also bought most of the Italian's surviving drawings and brought them back with him to England.

As a result of Jones' enthusiasm for Palladio, English architecture was transformed. The Classical style was introduced, and the burgeoning decorative vocabulary of Tudor architecture was banished. Gone were the turrets and bay windows: façades became much plainer and shallow roofs were hidden behind parapets. The Classical orders (Doric, Ionic,

Palladian

Walls: Rigorously symmetrical elevations; lower floors with rustication (massive blocks separated by deep joints); upper floors with attached Classical columns or pilasters; parapets

Roofs: Flat, concealed behind parapet

Ceilings: Panelled; often decorated with plasterwork and inserted paintings

Windows: Rectangular; topped with curved or triangular pediments

Doorways: Elaborately carved interior door surrounds

Pillars and columns: Classical orders

Decorative details: Derived from Italian Renaissance and ancient Roman architecture

Corinthian, Tuscan, and Composite) provided sets of rules for the design of columns, capitals, and other details. The buildings of Jones, such as the Queen's House at Greenwich, St Paul's church, Covent Garden (p59) and the long-vanished Prince's Lodging at Newmarket Palace, became models that were copied and varied by architects over the years. Jones had numerous followers and imitators and, if some of them did not grasp as clearly as he the conventions of Classical architecture, many of their buildings exhibited the strong Italian influence that won them the name Palladian.

With its perfectly symmetrical façade, Ionic columns, and box-like shape, the Queen's House, Greenwich, designed by Inigo Jones, was severely Classical, and the first house in England to be built in this style.

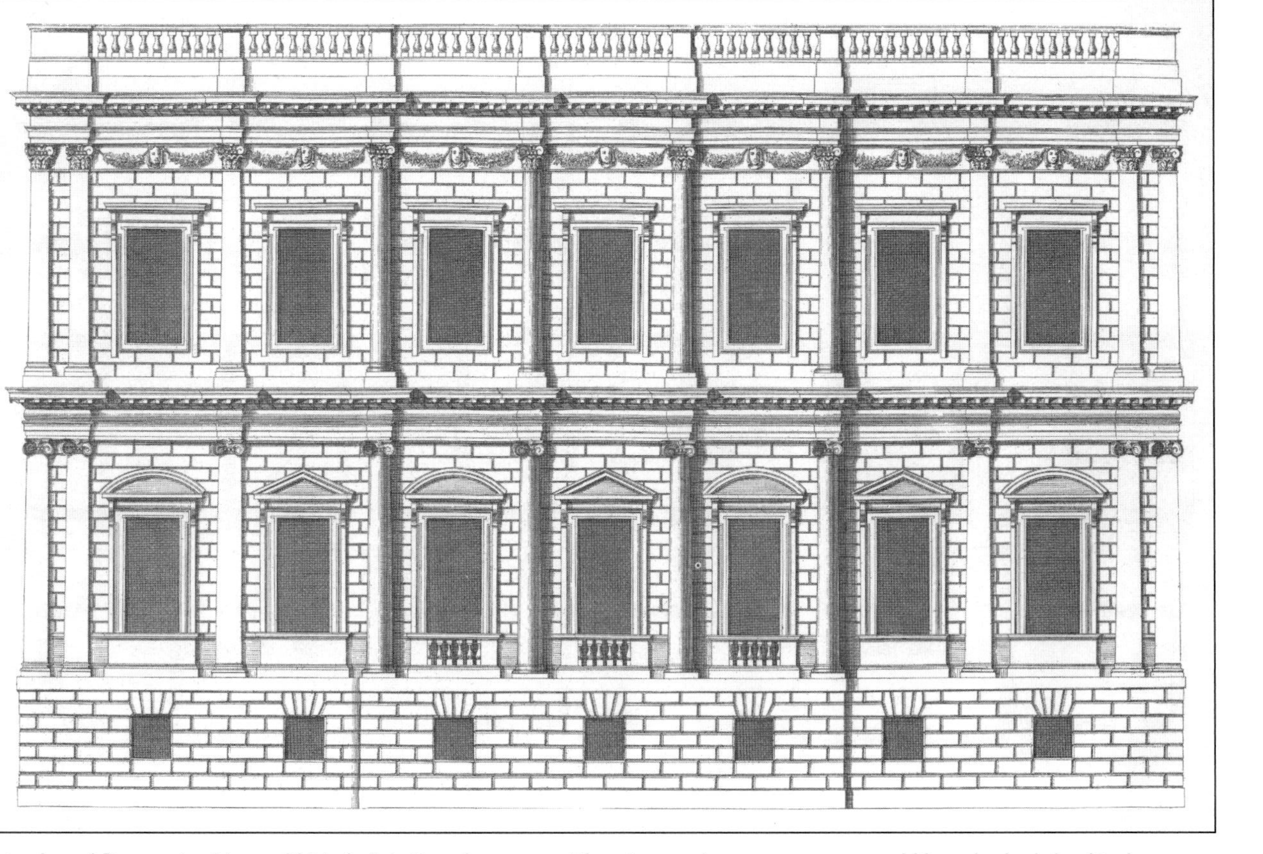

Inigo Jones' Banqueting House, Whitehall, built to house royal functions and court masques, would have looked shockingly different when built in the early-Seventeenth Century in a London full of brick and timber-framed buildings.

The simplest façade, reminding some of an Etruscan temple, marks Inigo Jones' church, St Paul's, Covent Garden, London. The small tower does not survive.

The great Double-Cube Room at Wilton House is one of the most stunning interiors of the Seventeenth Century. Perfectly proportioned, it boasts rich carving and panelling and an elaborate fireplace.

This is one of Inigo Jones' most dramatic designs, the York Stairs to the Thames on the embankment, London. The bold masonry and columns influenced many other architects in the design of gateways and lodges.

Wren and the English Baroque c. 1660–c. 1720

NOT ALL architects wanted to keep to the confines of Palladianism. In the second half of the Seventeenth Century as English architecture began to flex its muscles and break some of the Classical rules. This tendency is seen in the work of Sir Christopher Wren, who developed a much-imitated style of house-building with brick façades, hipped roofs, and dormer windows that proved popular in country and manor houses for the rest of the century. Wren was still more adventurous in the many churches he built in the capital after the Great Fire of London (1666). These churches are Classical in overall style and many are simple boxes of brick. But, when funds allowed, Wren crowned them with elaborate steeples, all different and all strikingly original in form, like Gothic spires reinterpreted for a Classical era.

Wren's followers, Nicholas Hawksmoor and Sir John Vanbrugh, developed this new way of building still further. They brought to English architecture a fresh sense of high drama – heavy masses, spectacular skylines, and ambitious scale are the keynotes of their buildings and this

Wren and the English Baroque

Walls: On houses: plain brick with central pediment, contrasting quoins. On churches: with Classical details including pilasters

Roofs: On houses: pitched, hipped, with dormer windows

Windows: Rectangular, sometimes topped with pediments; Venetian arch motif (central round-topped opening flanked by rectangular openings)

Doorways: With ornate surrounds and pediments

Columns: Classical

Decorative details: Different-shaped pediments; elaborate scrolls and other curved motifs; parapets with urns; elaborate church steeples

vastness is underlined in details like pronounced keystones in arches and big quoins, at the corners. Hawksmoor's churches, such as St George in the East, London, and Vanbrugh's vast and grandiose country houses, such as Blenheim Palace (p66) and Castle Howard, exemplify what this architecture is about. It is a style that has been called Baroque, although it lacks the curving walls and exuberant decoration that baroque buildings have in Italy or Central Europe. It is *English* Baroque – grand, but more grounded and solid, less airy, than the European variety.

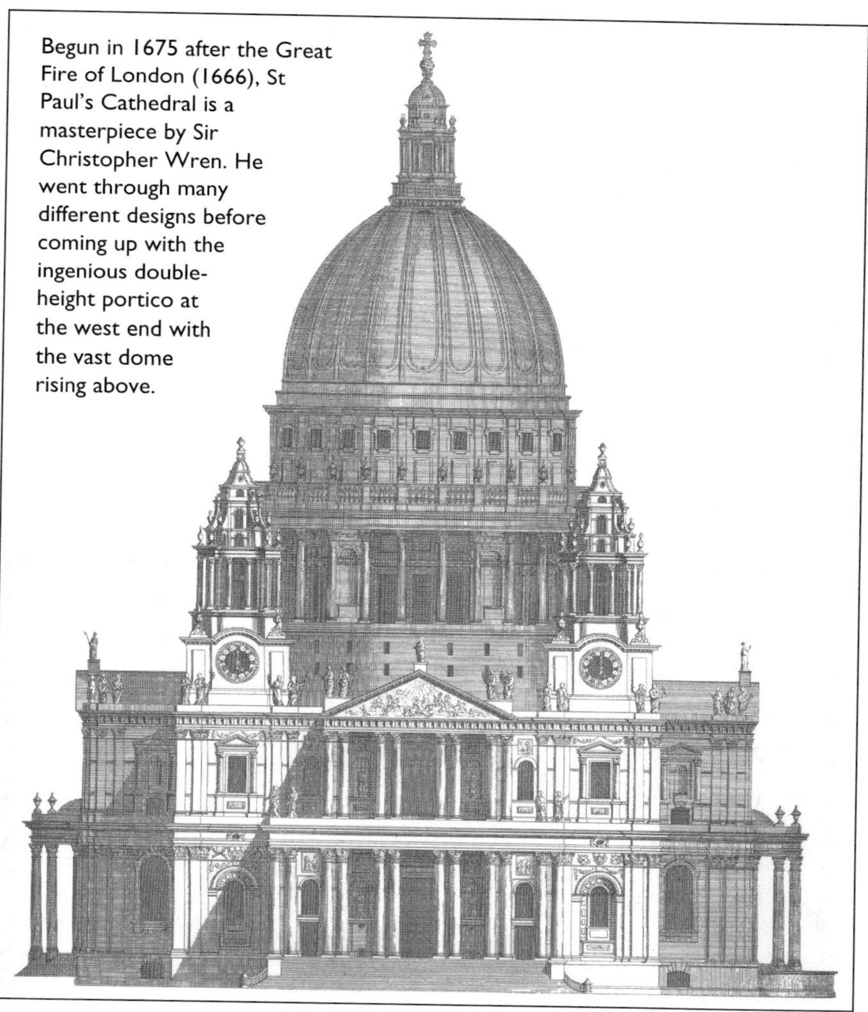

Begun in 1675 after the Great Fire of London (1666), St Paul's Cathedral is a masterpiece by Sir Christopher Wren. He went through many different designs before coming up with the ingenious double-height portico at the west end with the vast dome rising above.

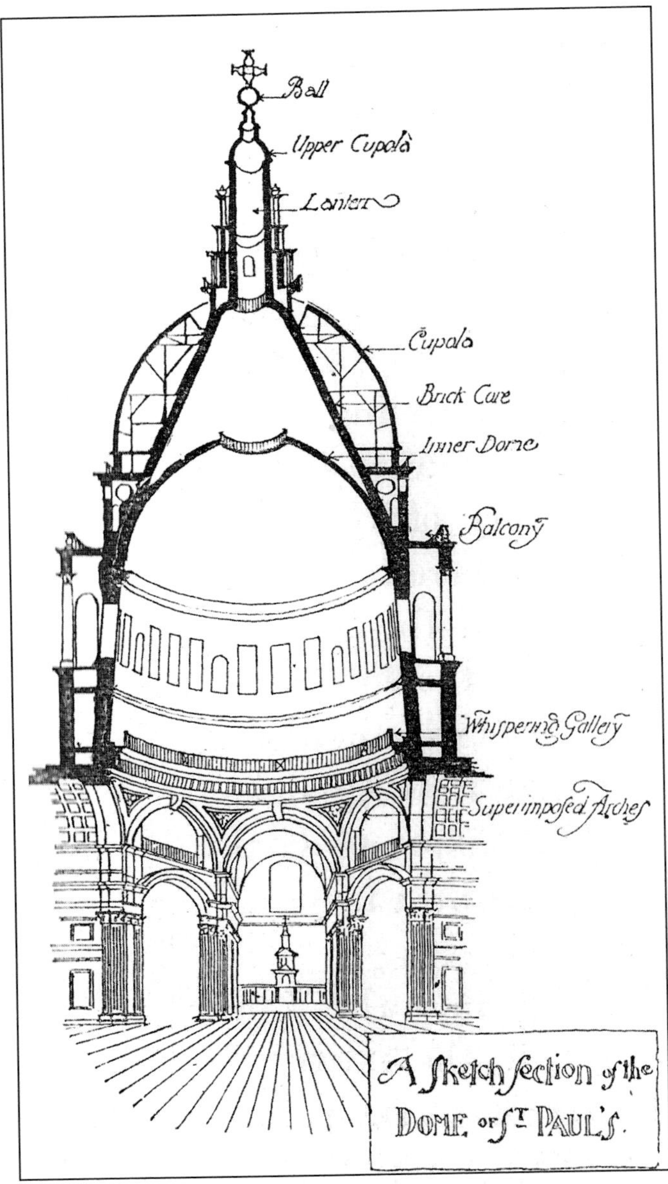

A section through the dome of St Paul's Cathedral shows how Wren ingeniously incorporated a cone of brick to support the tall lantern, whilst introducing an inner dome to provide a ceiling.

At Christ Church, Oxford, Wren designed the entrance tower, known as Tom Tower, to complement the Gothic architecture of the rest of the college.

Blenheim Palace, Oxfordshire, was the house designed by Sir John Vanbrugh for the Duke of Marlborough. Everything is on a vast scale – from big blocks of masonry to towering chimneys – and the grandeur is reflected by the proportions of the rooms inside.

This pavilion is one of the more Baroque parts of the Royal Naval Hospital at Greenwich. The theatrical effect is enhanced by statuary and gigantic columns.

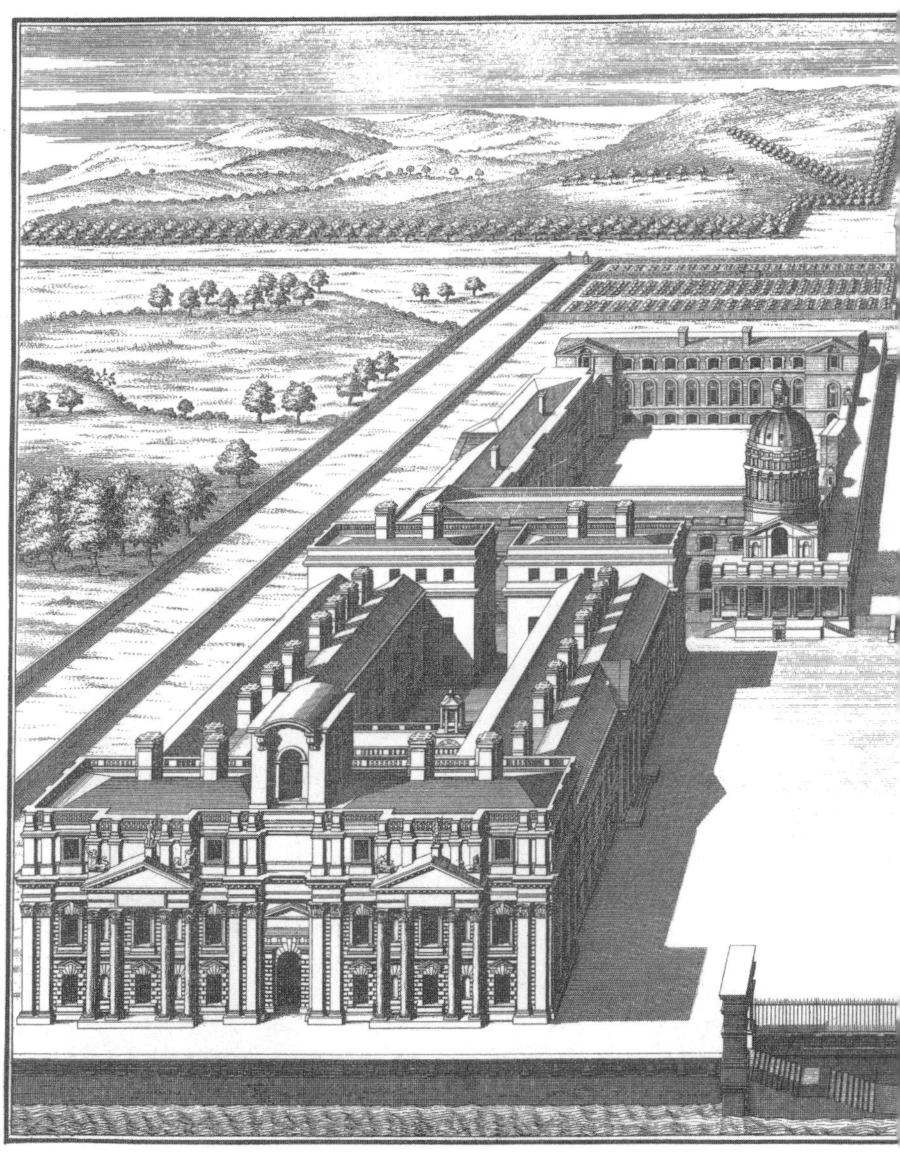

Wren, Hawksmoor, and Vanbrugh all contributed to the design of the enormous Royal Naval Hospital at Greenwich. Vast vistas open up between the buildings, and grand interiors include the Hall with paintings by Thornhill.

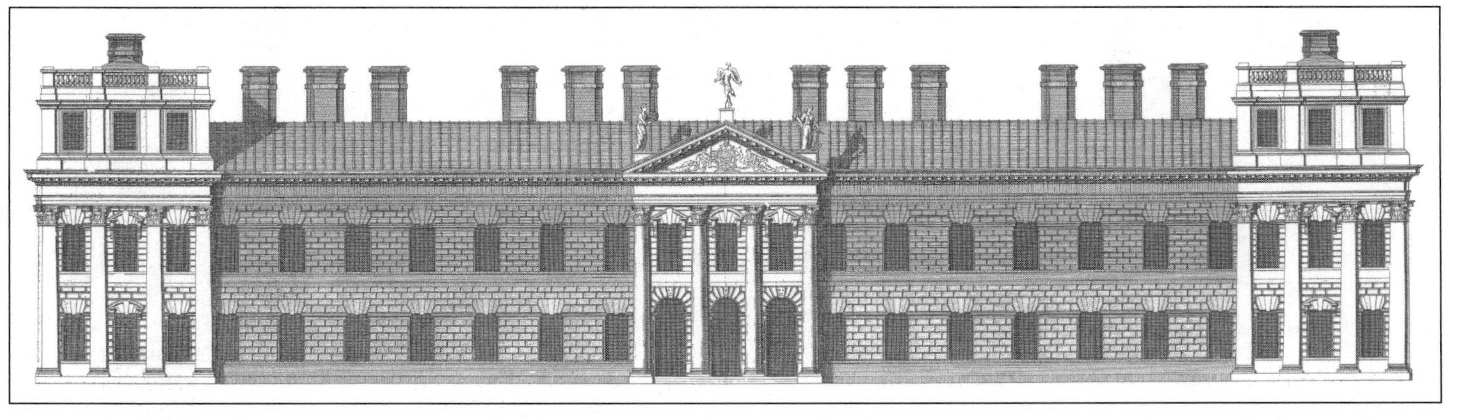

One wing of the Great Court of the Royal Hospital at Greenwich shows how the long rows of windows are punctuated by rows of columns and pilasters to break the monotony and increase the sense of scale.

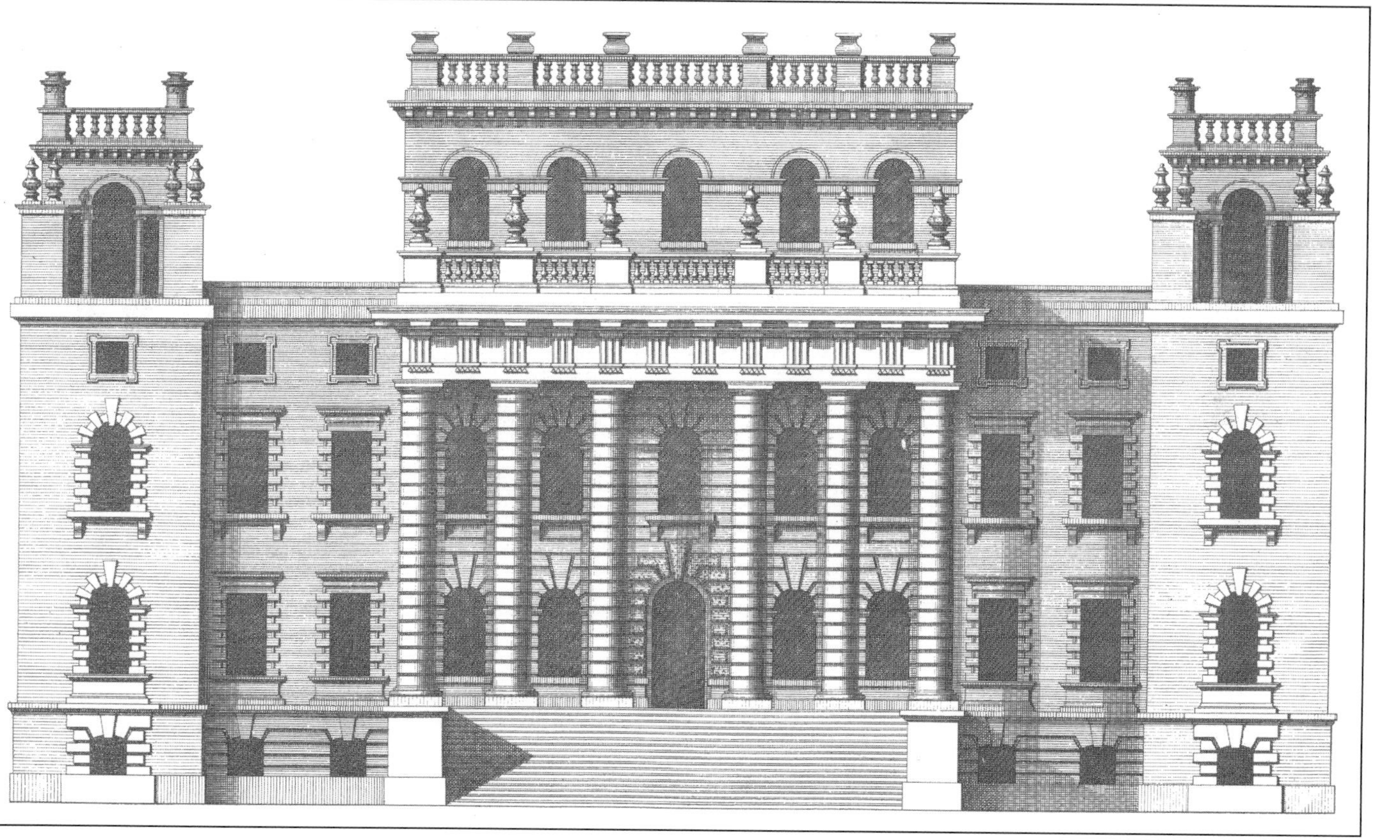

The bold use of rustication, in which the joints between the masonry blocks are exaggerated for effect, is a typical visual trick used by Sir John Vanbrugh in this façade at Eastbury, Dorset, a house that no longer stands.

This temple, a garden building by Vanbrugh at Eastbury, Dorset, has Classical columns and portico, but Baroque urns make the skyline more interesting.

Though smaller than Blenheim or Eastbury, Seaton Delaval, Northumberland, is not short of the drama that was Vanbrugh's trademark. The north front is full of interest, with several different shapes of window opening, together with turrets, urns, statues, and rustication.

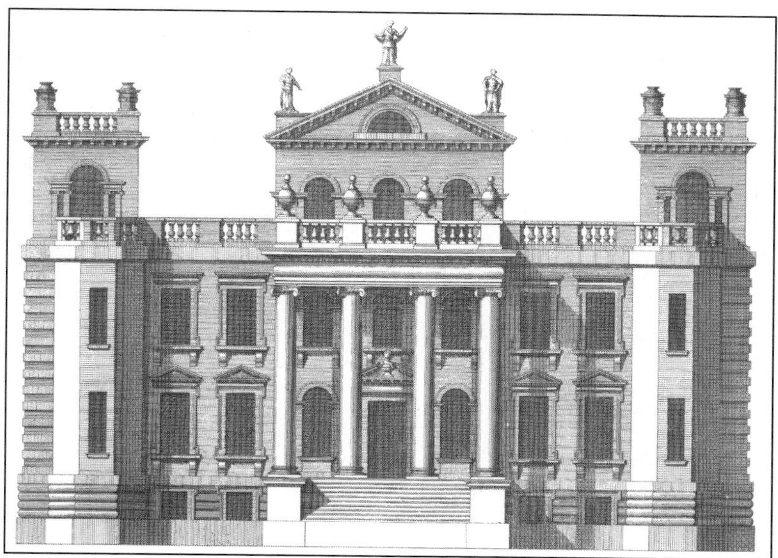

For the south front of Seaton Delaval, Vanbrugh marked the entrance with a row of Ionic columns.

More restrained than the work of Vanbrugh, the west front at Chatsworth gains its effect through its proportions and the use of carved details.

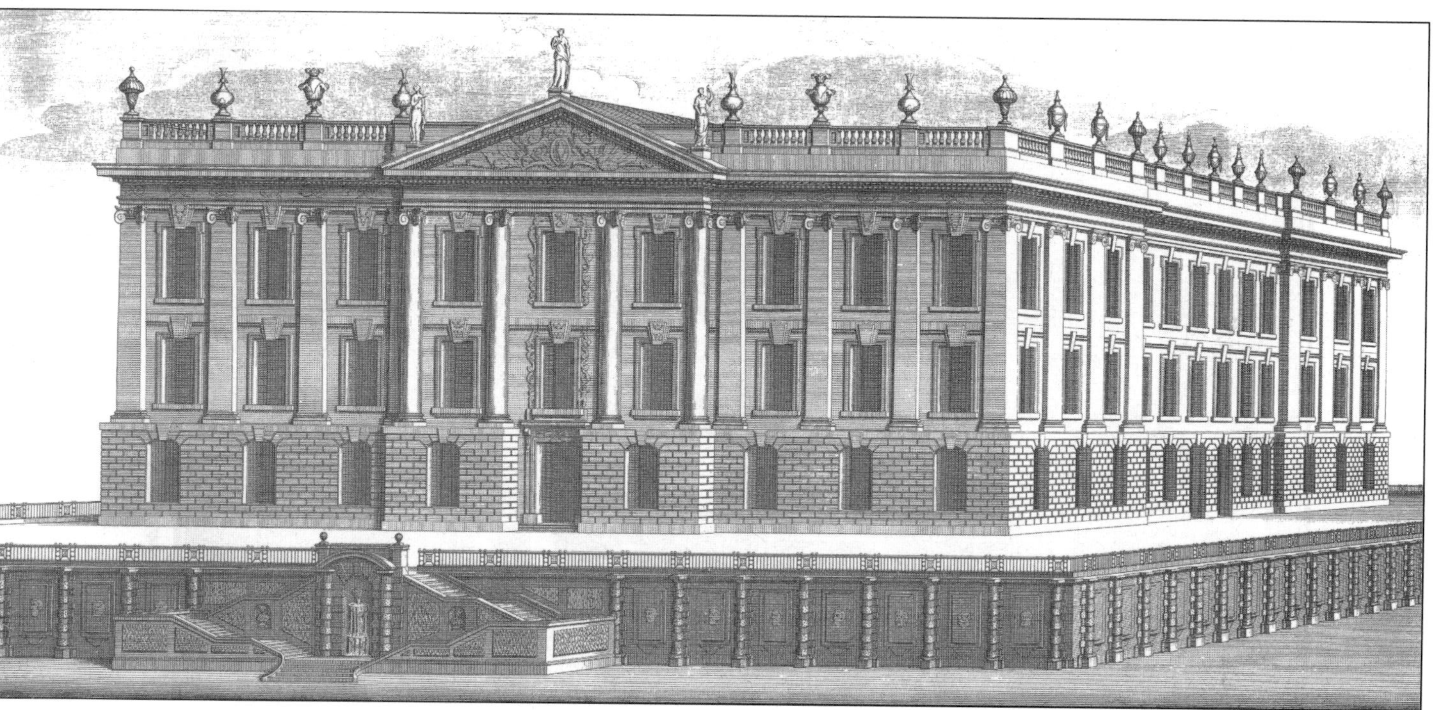

This view of Chatsworth shows the regular, Classical proportions of the house.

Interlude: The Terraced House

MORE down-to-earth was the most enduring architectural innovation of the period. The terraced house as we know it today began with speculative developments in London at the end of the Seventeenth Century. This very English form of house soon became common all over our cities and the Eighteenth Century was its heyday. Builders developed a basic formula – a 'vertical' house with services in the basement, living rooms on the lower floors, bedrooms above, and servants' rooms in the attic – and created a range of versions for all social and economic groups.

Even aristocrats would live in terraced houses if the buildings were grand enough, and the largest examples had plenty of big rooms, imposing columned porches and other status-aware details. Georgian builders extended their range down to the most basic and modest (the gamut extended from first to fourth-rate) and the terrace boom spread across London and provincial cities like Bath. The terraced house – adapting its details to prevailing fashions but remaining fundamentally the same – has been the epitome of English town-dwelling ever since.

Palladian Revival
c. 1715–c. 1760

FASHIONS in larger buildings moved faster. Vanbrugh's work as an architect spanned the years 1699 to his death in 1726. But, in 1715, before most of Vanbrugh's great country houses were completed, architectural fashion was already making another U-turn when Scottish architect Colen Campbell published the first volume of *Vitruvius Britannicus*, a collection of stunning engravings of British buildings that put forward the superiority of the Palladian style over the Baroque.

In the same year, Giacomo Leoni, a Venetian architect recently arrived in England, published the first part of his translation of Palladio's writings. These works in print were soon accompanied by works in stone: a Palladian revival was under way. Leoni's *Palladio* was a timely publication because the Eighteenth Century was a period when more and more rich Britons travelled to Europe, finding out about the art of France and Italy, and collecting works for their collections. This kind of artistic pilgrimage and shopping-spree, known as the Grand Tour, had an increasing influence on English art and architecture.

Campbell and Leoni were important Palladians, but Richard Boyle, 3rd Earl of Burlington was the most prominent Palladian of all. He designed

Palladian Revival

Walls: Rusticated lower storeys; columned entrance porticoes; pediments

Roofs: Shallow pitched or flat; sometimes with dome

Windows: Rectangular with pediments; Venetian

Columns: Classical

Decorative details: Imposing entrance staircases; ornate plasterwork; rich interiors with gilding, marble columns, ceilings coffered (with many rectangular inset panels)

Chiswick House for himself in the 1720s, and it became the hallmark Palladian building, based closely on the villas of Palladio himself. Square, white, and topped with a dome, it must have seemed like an alien invader on its green lawns outside London. It was certainly unlike any other English house except for Campbell's similar Mereworth Castle (p80).

Because Burlington was a prominent member of the aristocracy, news of his house travelled fast through the corridors of power. Soon, other nobles were building houses in the Palladian-style with plain walls, rusticated lower storeys, and pillared entrance porticoes; their rather austere exteriors contrasting with luxurious interiors filled with European art works and gilded furniture. William Kent, a protégé of Burlington who was, in turn, a landscape gardener, furniture designer, and architect, designed a number of these buildings, including the vast Holkham Hall for the agriculturalist Thomas Coke. Another of Kent's buildings was Horse Guards – which was in Whitehall, the very part of London where Palladianism had begun, back in the early-Seventeenth Century, with Inigo Jones' Banqueting House. Palladianism had come home.

Horse Guards was designed by William Kent but built in 1745–55 after his death. This view shows the arched entrance leading from Whitehall to the parade ground beyond.

The bagnio (bathhouse) in the gardens of Lord Burlington's Palladian villa at Chiswick, was designed by Burlington with the guidance of the architect Colen Campbell. As well as the basement bath, the building contained several living rooms.

Mereworth Castle, like Lord Burlington's Chiswick House, was based closely on an Italian villa designed by Palladio. It was built in 1722 to designs by Colen Campbell.

The Palladian elevation of Wittham, Somerset.

The 1751 Royal Exchange, was designed for the Lord Mayor of London (the Rt Hon St

James Bateman, Baronet) and since rebuilt.

Colen Campbell's first design for Wanstead House was a long building with a central portico. The house as completed is no longer standing.

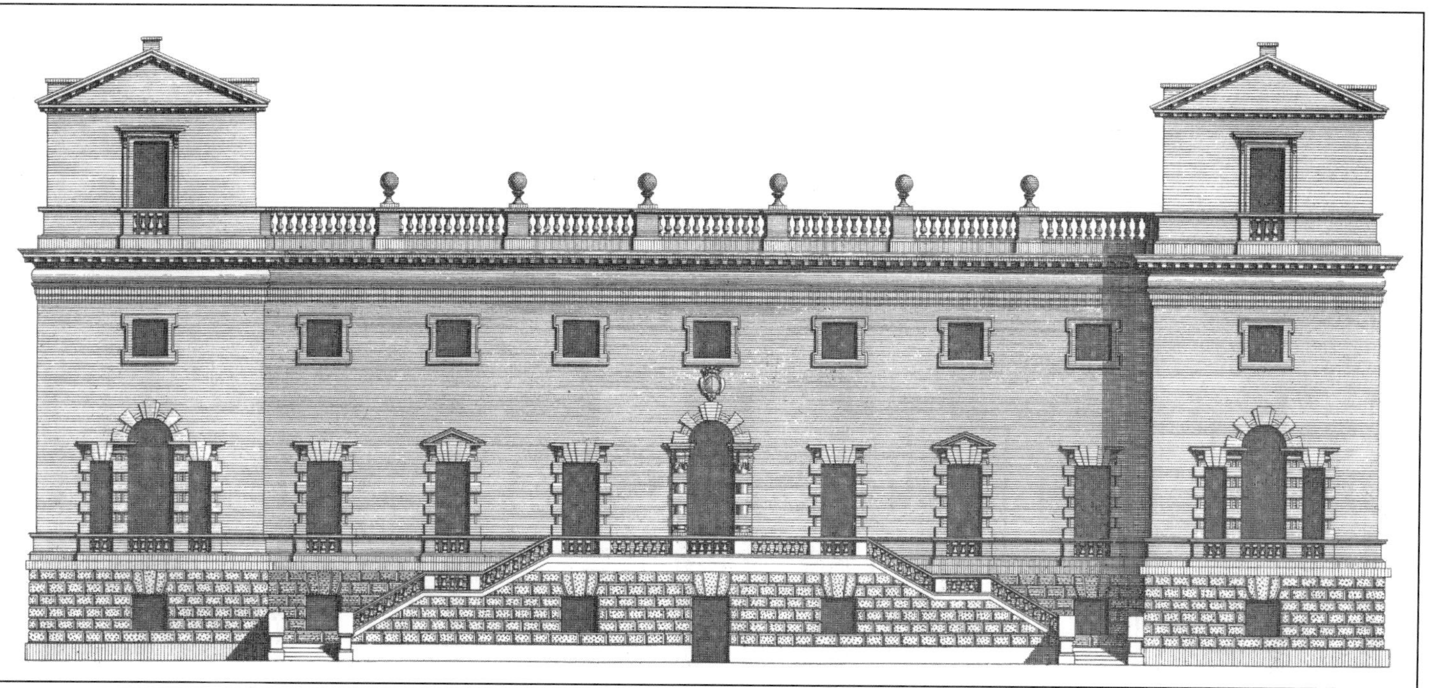

North front of Houghton Hall, Norfolk by Colen Campbell

Colen Campbell's design for the south front of Houghton Hall, Norfolk, includes a pair of corner towers influenced by the earlier Wilton House. These towers were later capped with small domes.

Althorp's long entrance front, with projecting wings on either side, has been much altered since this Eighteenth-century engraving was made, but still creates its effect by means of changing wall planes and a steady rhythm of sash windows.

Burlington House, Piccadilly by Colen Campbell: an additional storey was added later.

A view of Althorp showing the two projecting side wings.

Neo-Classicism c. 1760–c. 1790

GRAND, chaste, and rather forbidding, the buildings of Burlington and Kent were Classical structures – but this was Classicism seen through the lenses of Palladio, the Renaissance, and Inigo Jones. But what about the real buildings of ancient Greece and Rome? By the mid-Eighteenth Century, they were being rediscovered. Two British architects, James Stuart and Nicholas Revett, travelled through Greece and Asia Minor in the early 1750s, measuring and drawing the ancient buildings. In 1762, the fruits of their labours began to be published in the first volume of their *Antiquities of Athens*.

This book, which earned one of its authors the nickname James 'Athenian' Stuart, was part of a wider movement to appreciate the ruins of the ancient world. Robert Adam and Sir William Chambers were two other important architects who travelled abroad, both to Paris and Italy. The result was a greater variety of styles, many of which were neo-Classical. Chambers, for example, could design in the Palladian manner, but also took to a more French vision of neo-Classicism, with façades that featured plenty of decorative sculpture, including carved friezes and statues along parapets. This was a more delicate way to build than the Palladian style.

Robert Adam, too, espoused delicacy, especially in famous interiors of the 1760s and 1770s, such as those at Syon House and Osterley House,

Neo-Classicism

Walls: Plain, sometimes with giant pilasters

Windows: Rectangular, with plain surrounds

Doorways: Flanked by Classical columns, topped with fanlights

Columns: Classical, especially based on ancient Greek models

Decorative details: Classical motifs, e.g. acanthus leaf, anthemion (honeysuckle), Greek key. Also motifs such as swags, draped Classical figures, mythical beasts. Pastel interiors with cameo-like medallions in white

which are heavily influenced by ancient Rome. Adam added elements from the Renaissance and the Etruscans, too, blending everything together and not forgetting to design items like furniture and carpets to provide a complete decorative scheme. Circling and swirling sprigs of foliage, Classical motifs like the anthemion (honeysuckle) decoration, and reliefs of urns and vases run along friezes and across plaster ceilings. Pastel shades and white combine to make his interiors feel like vast Wedgwood vases. But there are also details picked out in gold. It is all the ultimate in refinement.

'Gothick' c. 1740–c. 1820

BUT WHILE architects like Adam and Chambers were extending the scope of English Classicism (and the Classicism of Adam's native Scotland), another group of designers and patrons were looking in a very different direction: back to the Gothic of the Middle Ages. Gothic had not lain dormant since the late-Fifteenth Century. There are a number of Gothic churches dating from the Sixteenth and Seventeenth Centuries and architects such as Hawksmoor were skilled exponents – Hawksmoor's towers for Westminster Abbey (p26) have fooled many visitors into thinking they are Medieval.

But Eighteenth-century Gothic was something different. Unlike the full-blown Gothic of the Middle Ages, Eighteenth-century Gothic was more about applying certain Medieval details – such as windows with Y-shaped tracery, battlements, and fan vaulting made not of stone but with plaster or papier mâché – to country houses and, sometimes, churches. As if to signal this 'applied' Medievalism, people began to spell the name of this style differently: it became 'Gothick'. The most famous example of this style was Strawberry Hill, Horace Walpole's house at Twickenham, which Walpole began building in Gothic, or Gothick, in 1747.

The form of Gothic pioneered by Walpole was delicate and fanciful.

Gothick

Walls: Buttressed, with battlements and turrets; asymmetrical façades

Ceilings: Fan and other Gothic styles of vaulting, often executed in plaster

Windows: Pointed or ogee-shaped, often with tracery in Y-form

Doorways: Pointed or ogee

Arches: Pointed

Columns: Gothic

Decorative details: Widespread use of most ornate Gothic-style features, e.g. niches, heraldic devices, stained glass, pinnacles, spirelets

Details were often based on authentic Medieval sources, but these sources could be used in bizarre combinations – a drawing room might contain features copied from two different Gothic cathedrals. What mattered was the overall effect, which was one of vaults as intricate as cake-icing, book-shelves topped with pointed arches like Medieval tomb recesses, heraldic panels, and stained glass glowing richly in candle-lit gloom.

Originally built c. 1803, in the Gothick style, Eaton Hall, Cheshire, was remodelled by the Victorians in a more correct Gothic Revival architecture. The house was demolished in 1961.

The Picturesque and the Exotic c. 1760–c. 1815

THE FANCIFUL Gothick was one of the styles taken up by the Picturesque movement in design, which tried to make gardens and houses look like elements in old master paintings, and which became fashionable after 1794, when Uvedale Price's *Essay on the Picturesque* was published. Well-heeled followers of the Picturesque liked gardens that featured eye-catchers such as mock-Medieval ruins. They also built cottages in varied and irregular style (sometimes with thatched roofs shaped like cottage loaves, sometimes with verandas held up by tree trunks) on their estates, bizarre buildings often called *cottages ornés*. As for their houses, these might be Gothic in style, but if they were Classical, they were Classical with a Picturesque spin, with irregular plans, asymmetrical façades and features such as a round tower at one corner. The master of this style, who designed both *cottages ornés* and asymmetrical Classical villas, was John Nash.

So the architecture of the late-Eighteenth and early-Nineteenth centuries – the late Georgian and Regency periods – was very varied, and this variety could sometimes take off in still less predictable directions.

The Picturesque

Walls: Vernacular style, using traditional materials (e.g. coursed rubble masonry, timber framing); asymmetrical façades and plans; porches; where Classical details are used, these are also arranged asymmetically

Roofs: Thatched or other vernacular styles, often generously overhanging

Windows: Varied; frequent use of bay windows; leaded lights; dormers common

Decorative details: Drawn from rustic Gothic or vernacular architecture; large or ornate chimneys

This was in keeping with the times, which were exemplified by the Prince Regent – George III's son, who became George IV in 1820 – who lived for pleasure and extravagance and whose greatest creation was the Royal Pavilion at Brighton, where Indian-style onion domes roof a decadent pleasure palace by the sea.

The exotic emerged in odd places. That great neo-Classicist Sir William Chambers, for example, was the most travelled of all architects of his time. He had even been to China, where he studied pagodas and, in 1756, he published *Designs for Chinese Buildings*. Some of his most impressive structures were the garden buildings, ranging in style from Classical to Moorish and Chinese, that he erected in Kew Gardens. The pagoda of 1761 is the most impressive of all.

The Prince Regent's Brighton Pavilion was designed by John Nash and built between 1815 and 1821 in a mixture of Indian and Chinese styles.

The interiors of Brighton Pavilion draw on a huge range of oriental motifs. In the dining room dragons, phoenixes, pagodas, and Chinese figures combine to adorn the walls, chandeliers, and other fittings.

Classical Revivals c. 1790–c. 1830

FOR MANY people in the late-Eighteenth and early-Nineteenth Centuries, Classicism was still the preferred style and, around 1800, it was revivified once more. This was partly the work of master-architects like Sir John Soane, whose architecture of shallow domes, semicircular or segmental windows, and intricate interior vistas was drawn partly from the fantasy engravings of the Italian artist Piranesi. Soane became famous as the architect of the Bank of England and of numerous houses and churches. Joseph Bonomi, himself born in Italy, was another Classical master of the late-Eighteenth Century. His strong European neo-Classicism was popular with country-house clients.

Designers like Soane and Bonomi were individualists, but their work prepared the way for a more widespread Greek revival, when architects in the first 30 years or so of the Nineteenth Century began to design in a much more purely archaeological Greek style. The continuing series of Stuart and Revett's volumes of *Antiquities of Athens*, which appeared slowly (Volume II came out in 1787/89, Volume III in 1795, and a further volume in 1816), helped fuel interest in the Greek style. So did the work

Classical Revivals

Walls: Sometimes with giant pilasters, sometimes with niches, balconies, and other ornate details

Windows: A variety of forms: rectangular, with plain surrounds; round-headed; Venetian; oval or circular

Doorways: Behind large Classical porticoes

Columns: Classical

Decorative details: Classical motifs, e.g. acanthus leaf, anthemion (honeysuckle), Greek key. Relief carvings or moulding in pediments. Also statuary, urns, and ornate parapets

of men like William Wilkins, who had the chance to apply the style to various important houses and public buildings. With rows of columns supporting entablatures that concealed shallow-pitched roofs, these buildings looked more like Grecian temples than earlier Classical buildings in England. It was a sombre style, but one well suited to structures like the Shire Hall in Norwich and London's National Gallery. Greek seemed established as *the* style for public buildings.

London's Marble Arch was built to an 1820s design by Nash. It is based on Roman triumphal arches and the architect originally intended that it should have more sculpture, including a statue of Victory on top.

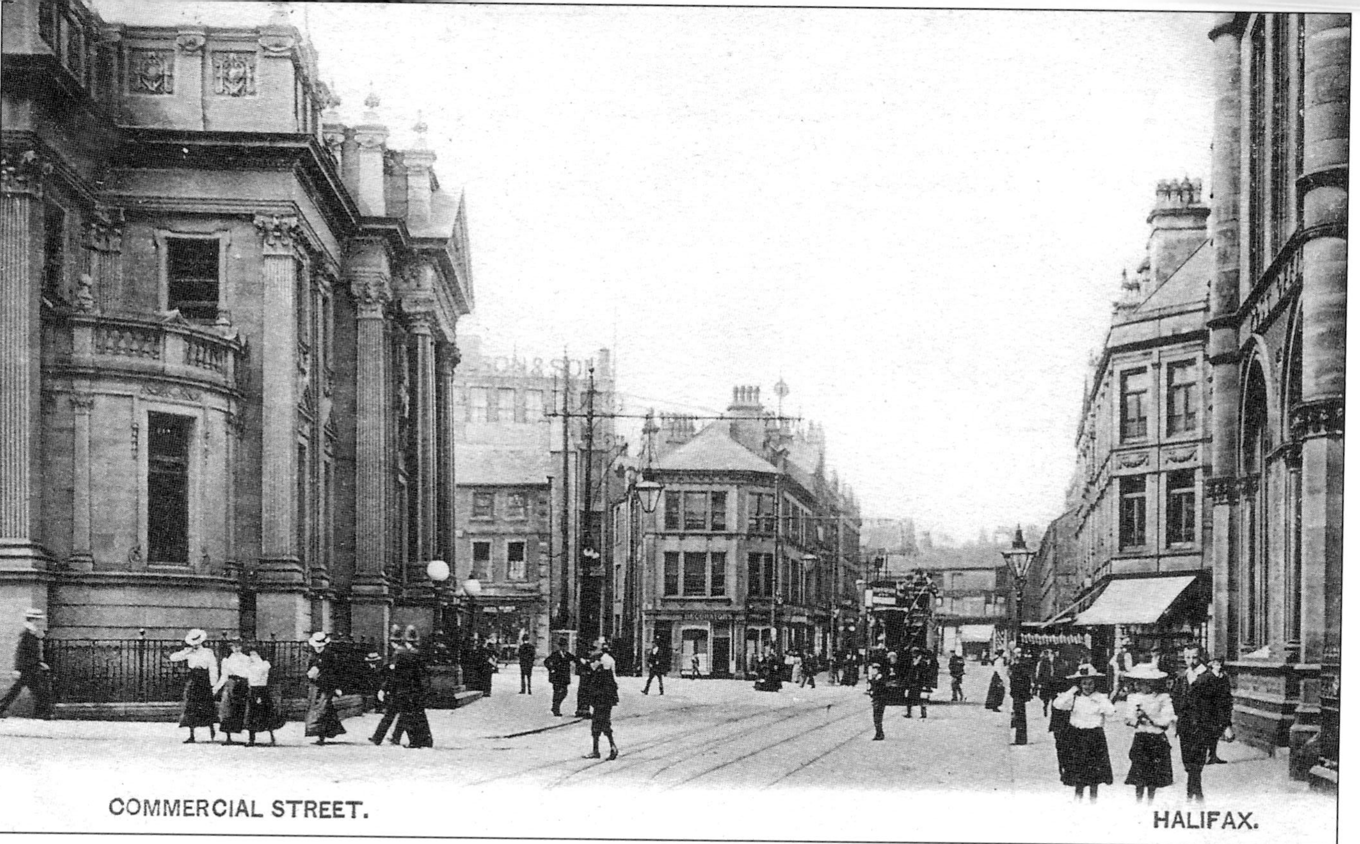

Buildings with Classical detailing line Commercial Street, Halifax, in this Edwardian postcard. Many prosperous northern towns adopted the Classical style for public buildings.

Interlude: The Industrial Revolution c. 1770–c. 1850

FOR HUNDREDS of years, 'major buildings' meant large churches, country houses, or the occasional manifestation of civic pride like a town hall or market house. But, in the Eighteenth Century, life began to change in England with the coming of industry, and architecture changed with it. The factory system evolved when entrepreneurs like Joseph Arkwright of Cromford realised that they could produce goods more cheaply and efficiently by mechanising the production process. And mechanisation meant bringing hundreds of workers under one roof to operate powered machinery. The age of the factory had arrived.

Factory architecture derived largely from the architecture of water mills, which often had a number of floors held up by ranks of wooden posts and lit by rows of windows. A water wheel at one end provided power for the machinery. Factories were similar, but soon grew larger. As major buildings owned by manufacturers who wanted to make a statement, early factories were sometimes adorned with Classical details (attached columns on either side of the door, for example) but they were largely plain – these were working structures first and foremost and their job was to turn a profit. But these buildings were structurally and architecturally influential. The basic formula – multiple floors, columns, and so on – was good for warehouses as well as factories; later it was adapted for office blocks too. And when builders learnt how to make their structures fireproof by using iron columns and brick-arched ceilings, they paved the way for the building held up entirely by a framework of columns and beams – the skyscraper.

Of the most notable early factory buildings, Arkwright's first mill at Cromford – built in 1771 and arguably the world's first factory – set the style. Factories such as Quarry Bank Mill at Styal (1784) pioneered fireproof construction in metal and brick. But the most forward-looking of all early industrial buildings was Marshall, Benyon and Bage's flax mill of 1796 at Ditherington, Shrewsbury, the first building in the world to be constructed with a metal frame.

Gothic Revival c. 1830–c. 1890

IN THE 1830s, architects began to look more seriously at Medieval Gothic buildings. They saw that it was possible to imitate Medieval Gothic much more closely than Walpole and his followers had done, and that a revived 'authentic' Gothic was an ideal style for the hundreds of churches that were needed in England's growing towns and cities. What was more, they saw how Gothic could be adapted for all sorts of buildings, including many kinds, from hotels to railway stations, that had not even existed in the Middle Ages.

Gothic encompassed several styles. Architects had Early English, Decorated, and Perpendicular to draw on for inspiration, as well as the varieties of Gothic that evolved in Continental Europe. Which version of Gothic was the one to choose? One of the first and greatest Victorian Gothic architects, A. W. N. Pugin, favoured Fourteenth-century Gothic, also known as Decorated or 'Second Pointed'. Ornate churches by Pugin and his followers developed this style, adding all the rich decorative details, such as wall paintings and stained glass, that had largely vanished from the original churches of the Fourteenth Century. Entering a church like this is like being inside a jewel casket – it is dark, but everything gleams.

But Decorated was not the only style. Charles Barry and Pugin used a sort of Perpendicular-Tudor hybrid for the Houses of Parliament and a number of other architects built Perpendicular-style churches in the early-Victorian period. In the early 1850s, people began to appreciate the virtues of brickwork and to see how it could be used in Gothic structures. The buildings of William Butterfield, like All Saints, Margaret Street, London, led the way, their multi-coloured brick colourful and bold. Critic and writer John Ruskin, writing passionately about Venetian Gothic in books such as *Stones of Venice* (1851), added to the enthusiasm for brick. Venetian Gothic also proved adaptable for industrial and commercial buildings and warehouses that look like the Doge's Palace sprang up. For other designers, such as J. L. Pearson, Early English Gothic was a source of deep inspiration. Elegant vaulted churches like his St Augustine, Kilburn and the Church of St Peter, Vauxhall (p109), were the result.

None of these architects were slavish imitators. They all added to and extended Medieval Gothic. But some went still further, inventing forms, from madly carved wooden roofs, to outlandishly painted walls, that were radically different from anything produced in the Middle Ages. These designers had the audacity to stretch Gothic in new directions, incorrect and feverishly inventive. The Twentieth-century architect H. S. Goodhart-Rendel called them 'rogue architects' and their architecture, with its jazzy patterns and manically criss-crossing roof timbers, is as large and loud as a trumpeting tusker.

Perhaps more admirable, and ultimately more inventive, were the builders who adapted Gothic to new or recent building types. Government buildings, law courts, company headquarters, stations, factories, and pump houses – from high status to low, Gothic seemed able to conquer all forms. There was no precedent, for example, for a town hall on the scale of Manchester's, and Alfred Waterhouse's use of Gothic for its design is a triumph at every level. The seemingly endless variations in arches and windows allow the building to fit a difficult site perfectly, and to turn awkward corners with turrets and bays. The internal planning is masterly. And the decoration, with carvings and mosaics in tribute to Manchester's mercantile success, fits the bill.

Gothic Revival

Walls: Full range of Gothic features, including buttresses, large pointed windows, pinnacles, etc.

Windows: Each of the three Gothic tracery styles proved popular with different architects

Decorative details: Polychrome brickwork; coloured wall- and floor-tiles; ornate ironwork; stained glass; the full repertoire of Gothic ornament

Architects Charles Barry and A. W. N. Pugin used a version of Gothic from the late-Fifteenth or early-Sixteenth Century for the Houses of Parliament, begun in 1835. Barry designed most of the exterior, Pugin created the interiors and designed the famous clock tower, popularly known as Big Ben.

The Roman Catholic Abbey of St Scholastica, Teignmouth, was designed in 1863 by architect George Goldie in the early Gothic style.

The young architect Benjamin Woodward designed Oxford's University Museum in 1854. He based the adjoining chemistry laboratory, on the right, on the Medieval kitchen at Glastonbury Abbey.

Balliol College, Oxford, expanded hugely in the 1860s using designs by Alfred Waterhouse. He used varying heights to give the buildings a similar feel to the university's Medieval buildings.

(left) Balliol College Chapel was built to an 1856 design by William Butterfield. The architect's love of using different-coloured bricks and stones is clear.

(right) The chapel at Exeter College, Oxford, was designed by George Gilbert Scott and built in 1856–59. It is a soaring Gothic building, with tall windows, doorway, and buttresses.

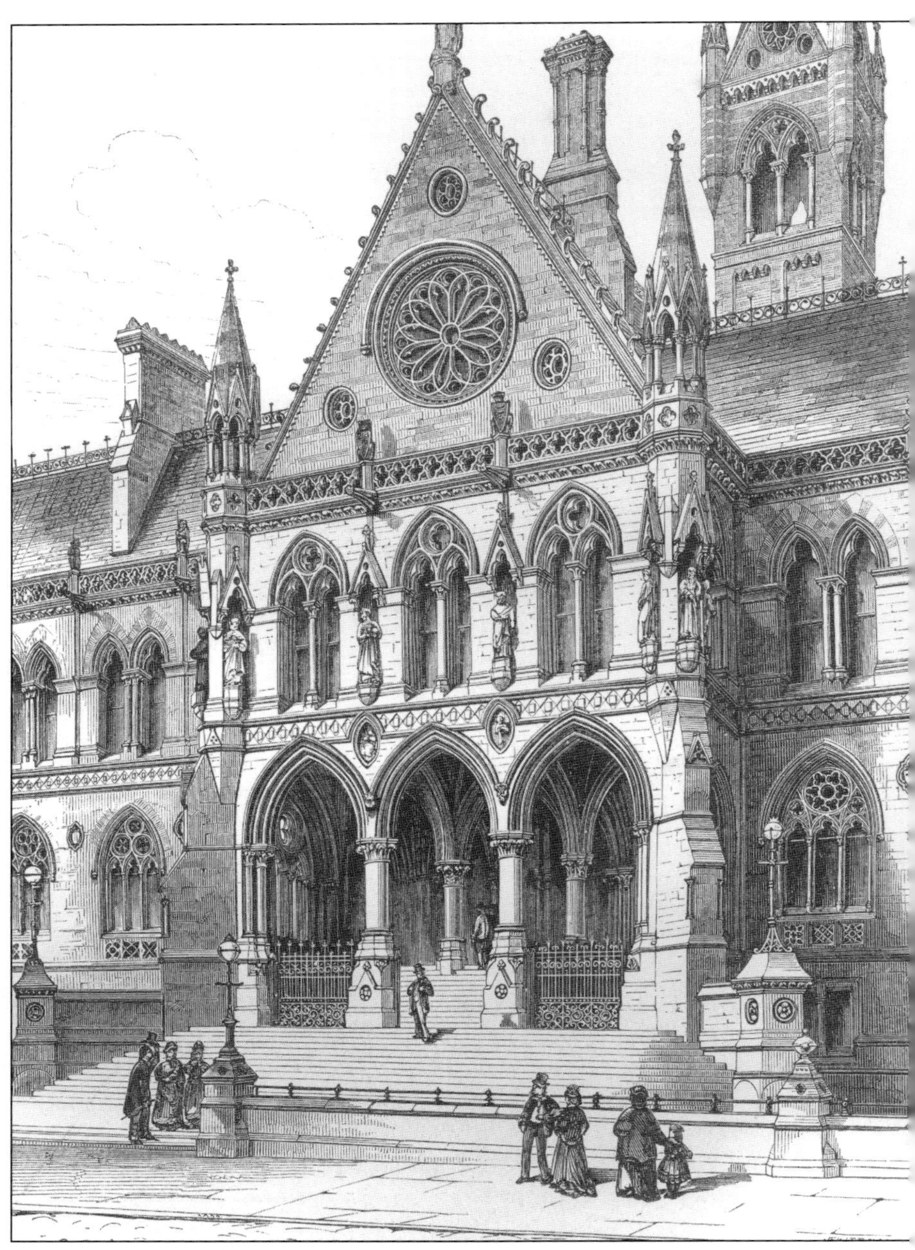

Alfred Waterhouse's 1859 Assize Courts at Manchester were in an elaborate Gothic style with rich carving and statuary. The building was bombed in World War II and later replaced, but some of the statues can still be seen in the modern court buildings.

Architects Hadfield and Weightman were influenced by Decorated Gothic in their 1845 design for the Roman Catholic cathedral at Salford. Some of the details are based on the Fourteenth-century choir of Selby Abbey.

The spire of St Mary's, Chetwynde, Shropshire, dating from 1865 and designed by the architect R. Ferry, draws on the Early English Gothic style.

John Loughborough Pearson created a rich interior and vault in St Peter's, Vauxhall, 1863. Fine carvings, stained glass, and wall paintings surround the high altar.

Rich decoration, including multi-coloured masonry and carved tracery, enlivens the chancel of St John's, Torquay, designed by George Edmund Street in 1869.

Interlude: Iron and Glass c. 1836–c. 1865

THE VICTORIANS were adept at developing new technologies, and their use of iron and glass in building is an example of this ability that transformed architecture. Joseph Paxton, an inspired gardener-turned-engineer who designed greenhouses, enlarged on this skill to produce the Crystal Palace, the great iron and glass hall originally built to house the 1851 Great Exhibition in Hyde Park. Paxton developed greenhouse-building techniques to deliver the Crystal Palace at speed, using prefabrication.

The Crystal Palace was a triumph and showed the scope of iron and glass. In the 1850s and 1860s, it was followed by a series of railway termini with great arching train sheds, buildings that showed still more lastingly the effectiveness of this kind of construction. Structures like King's Cross, Paddington, and St Pancras stations are still used for their original purpose, each a powerful reminder of Victorian foresight and engineering ability. The recently restored St Pancras, in particular, shows off Nineteenth-century engineering skill to great advantage.

On a smaller scale, the shopping arcade and market hall proved ideal for glass construction too. Many is the growing city, from Leeds to London, that still boasts Victorian markets or arcades with glass roofs flooding light on to the goods below. But the use of these materials went further. Following the lead both of early factory builders and of Victorians like Paxton, the architects of the Twentieth Century were to base countless office towers on prefabricated frames. They all have their origins in the endeavours of the architects and engineers of the Victorian period and earlier.

The sheer size of the Crystal Palace exhibition hall amazed the Victorians, but this was achieved by using repeating, mass-produced elements that could be brought to the site and assembled at speed.

When it was built in 1866–68, the train shed at London's St Pancras Station was, at 245 ft across, the widest roof span in the world. It was the brainchild of engineer W. H. Barlow and has recently been magnificently restored.

Victorian Variety c. 1840–c. 1900

THE EXTRAORDINARY range of Nineteenth-century Gothic, from Early English to Perpendicular, and from humble cottage to vast town hall, was typical of the Victorians. They built more, and more diversely, than any people before. Cities were expanding, London was the heart of a world empire, and technology was developing at breakneck speed, bequeathing builders projects as diverse as exhibition halls and sewers. Confidence was natural to the Victorians, and they soon extended their grasp of a host of architectural styles.

Italian Renaissance water towers, Germanic concert halls, Classical libraries, museums in the Romanesque style, French Renaissance hotels – these are just some of the joys of Victorian architecture in addition to the vast numbers of Gothic buildings.

Then there was the predilection for earlier English modes. One of these was a style, often known as 'Old English', a mixture of stone and timber-framing with lots of irregular turrets and windows, that was perfected by R. Norman Shaw for use on some large country houses, such as Cragside. Like Gothic, it drew on the Victorians' love of English history and the way they liked to identify with their ancestors. It went with mock-tournaments and suits of armour in the hall.

More widespread, and more popular for smaller houses in towns, was the style named 'Queen Anne'. This was a fashion that developed in partial imitation of late-Seventeenth-century domestic architecture, with its fine brickwork, generous pale stone dressings, decorative, Dutch-looking gables, and attractive window openings often featuring bays. Many Victorians, mindful of the religious tone of Gothic, saw it as a useful style for commercial and domestic buildings, enabling the pointed style to be reserved for churches. Light, versatile, and urbane, Queen Anne caught on widely, and was used for houses, schools, and shops, amongst other buildings. A 'Flemish' variant, with still more ornate gables and decorations, grew out of it.

Built in 1860–65, St Philip and St James, Oxford, was modelled by architect George Edmund Street on French churches of the Thirteenth Century with an abundance of lancet windows and an apsidal (curving) east end.

The Great Western Station Hotel, serving London's Paddington Station, is an example of the Victorian use of Classical architecture for a large building.

Arts and Crafts c. 1870–c. 1910

INTEREST IN Gothic, the development of the 'Old English' style and countless church restorations had given many Victorian architects a detailed understanding of traditional building techniques. In the 1860s, some of these architects, such as R. Norman Shaw and William E. Nesfield, started to build houses in styles close to the traditional vernacular. A number of younger architects took this pursuit up more single-mindedly, studying traditional buildings, joining societies such as the Art Workers' Guild and the Society for the Protection of Ancient Buildings, and trying to rid their own work of reliance on academic architectural styles.

The result was the Arts and Crafts movement in architecture and design. Many Arts and Crafts architects, such as C. F. A. Voysey and E. S. Prior, used local materials and based their details on the local vernacular. They allowed the plan and arrangement of the rooms in a house dictate the appearance of their façades. And they used ornament based largely on nature. They pursued an interest in building crafts, employing the best plasterers, carvers, and other workers that they could find. Their buildings, as a result, seem grounded in their locality, an effect which sweeping roofs and long, horizontal lines seem to emphasize.

There was another tendency in Arts and Crafts architecture, which

Arts and Crafts

Walls: Local materials or plain rendered surfaces; low walls; asymmetrical design with many elements such as bays and gables

Roofs: Broad roofs that sweep down to meet low walls

Windows: A variety of shapes and styles, including new tracery designs with roots in Gothic; dormers

Decorative details: Wooden panelling combined with pale plasterwork; carved beams; handcrafted details such as door furniture; large fireplaces sometimes in inglenooks; William Morris fabrics and wallpapers stressed the artistic side of the movement. Architects who followed this path could produce jewel-like interiors, sometimes based on Byzantine sources, with glittering mosaics and metalwork. It was a mode that proved successful in churches, but in the more restrained hands of architects such as Edwin Lutyens and Baillie Scott, also produced stunning domestic interiors. In their greatest buildings, such as Baillie Scott's house, Blackwell, the arts and the crafts come memorably together to produce some of the most striking rooms in the history of English architecture.

The Turn of the Century c. 1890–c. 1914

THE ARTS and Crafts movement added one more way of building to the plethora of styles – Gothic, neo-Jacobean, Italian Renaissance, Queen Anne – employed by the late Victorians. Towards the end of the Nineteenth Century, many architects tried to create a different style for larger buildings, by adapting historical features and using them in new ways. The new mode, varied and adaptable, became known as 'free design' or 'Free Style'.

Free Style buildings could draw on Jacobean details (mullioned windows, tall chimneys, ball finials), but might have Queen Anne elements (brickwork, stone dressings, sash windows, 'Dutch' gables), plus a touch of Scottish baronial (round corner turrets). They could be highly decorated, as in the work of Charles Harrison Townsend, designer of South London's Horniman Museum. But there were also plainer versions of the style, impressively massed, such as Bristol's Central Library, designed by a younger architect who was later to play a key role in the modern movement, Charles Holden.

Varied as it was, Free Style was only one side of Edwardian architecture. Edwardian Baroque, with its heavy rustication, thrusting towers, and prominent domes, was also a popular style, giving buildings such as town halls, banks, and major office developments the requisite sense of their own importance. Bigger and more monumental than anything the Seventeenth-century English Baroque produced, Edwardian Baroque buildings still dominate large areas of many major city centres. Their façades, often in shopping streets and little regarded by the shoppers below, are an over-the-top visual banquet. London's Piccadilly Hotel, designed by the versatile R. Norman Shaw, is a good example.

Interlude: Garden and Suburb c. 1870–c. 1920

TOWARDS the end of the Nineteenth Century, many architects and planners wanted to improve the living conditions of the working classes, especially the working classes who lived in cities. For many poor people, city life was grim. Rows of cramped houses had no proper sanitation, offered no privacy, and were relieved by neither gardens nor green spaces.

Social reformers like Dame Henrietta Barnett, wife of Canon Barnett who had worked with the poor in London's East End, had a different vision. Garden suburbs would provide more space, cleaner conditions, and, above all, a 'green' layout, with generous gardens and curving, tree-lined streets. They would also aim to avoid social ghettos, by persuading the middle and lower classes to live in the same neighbourhood.

The fruits of this vision were suburbs such as London's Bedford Park (1870s and 1880s) and Hampstead Garden Suburb (1905 onwards), developments that inspired many other housing schemes in the early-Twentieth Century. Although many of these later estates were neither as well designed nor as green as the early examples, they offered a better quality of life than the Victorian back-to-back houses that many of their residents had previously occupied.

The garden development idea was also taken further after the First World War, with the creation of garden cities – Letchworth and Welwyn Garden Cities. These set new standards for organised and people-friendly town planning. They are still popular places in which to live.

Modernism c. 1920–1939

IN THE 1920s and 1930s there was a huge change in English architecture, at least as far as the most progressive architects went. On the Continent, pioneers such as Walter Gropius developed an architecture in which ornament was banished and in which form, at least in theory, was dictated by the function of the building. In practice, this meant buildings with plain façades in which concrete, steel, and glass played the main roles. Flat roofs were the norm.

The most dazzling examples in England were a number of one-off houses – literally dazzling, since they were finished with brilliant white walls and strips of metal-framed windows – by architects such as Amyas Connell and Oliver Hill. Generous balconies (reflecting European ideas about the health-giving qualities of fresh air) and 'open' interior planning in which partition walls were kept to a minimum and one space merged into the next, were typical features.

Industrial buildings, like the Shredded Wheat factory at Welwyn Garden City, leant themselves well to this kind of architecture, as did public buildings, such as the striking De La Warr Pavilion in Bexhill-on-Sea by Mendelssohn and Chermayeff. This was shockingly new architecture, which most people thought was unlike anything that had gone before in England. But there were precedents from earlier decades, such as glass and metal buildings in Liverpool by Peter Ellis and flat-roofed factories and offices by Sellers and Wood. But none of these were as strikingly, aggressively modern as the brilliant white houses of the 1920s.

Modernism

Walls: Plain, white, rendered; sometimes raised on plain concrete columns called pilotis

Roofs: Flat, sometimes with roof terraces bounded by horizontal railings

Windows: Rectangular, often arranged together to form long horizontal bands of glazing

Doorways: Plain

Decorative details: Pronounced lack of ornament

Art Deco and 'Moderne' c. 1925–1939

BUT THE Modernist rejection of ornament was too much for many designers. New building types like cinemas seemed to cry out for a less tight-lipped style. They found it in Art Deco, a souped-up modern style in which all kinds of decoration, often very opulent, and references to the past, especially details drawn from ancient Egypt, tamed the white walls and made them look less stark. Soon, factory architects were adopting the style too, and some of the best surviving Art Deco buildings are factories, like the magnificent Carreras building (now called Greater London House) and the Hoover Building (now a supermarket), both in London. Both combine Egyptian motifs with contemporary decorative elements and both add bright colour to white façades.

Another way to tone down Modernism was to make the buildings less angular, sacrificing the doctrine of 'form follows function' by adding some curves. This produces the style known as 'Moderne', less colourful than Art Deco but more friendly than Modernism. Curving corners, bays with panes of glass that bend their way around, and the occasional circular

Art Deco and Moderne

Walls: Plain, pale rendered, sometimes relieved with shallow geometrical mouldings

Roofs: Flat, sometimes with roof terraces

Windows: Rectangular, metal-framed; bay windows sometimes make use of curved glass panes; stained glass sometimes used in smaller lights

Decorative details: Motifs drawn from Egyptian or, sometimes, Classical architecture; combination of curving corners and jagged edges; colourful geometrical designs above elements such as doorways; simple mouldings; geometrical effects; light-fittings, fireplaces, and other built-in elements using geometrical designs

window like a port hole, make Moderne houses and apartment blocks like bits of ocean liners. The watery theme was appropriate enough when this mode was used for many outdoor pools and lidos.

So, English architecture faced the outbreak of the Second World War in rude health, confronting the varied challenges of designing houses, factories, cinemas, and shops in its usual variety of ways. If many suburban houses were rather dull and predictable, the influence of the Garden Suburb movement was still beneficial in some public housing developments. Modernism seemed to offer a flexible way of designing anything from houses to warehouses. Art Deco added a splash of colour and humour. English builders and architects were doing what they do best – taking outside influences and giving them their own native twist and the world of English building seemed rich with variety and new possibilities. The tragedy and destruction of war brought this optimistic building boom to an end and, when rebuilding began in earnest after the war, English architecture took a different direction. The colourful world of Art Deco, the cottagey cosiness of the garden suburbs, and the stylistic variety of the pre-war decades were left behind.

Appendix One

Classical Columns

TUSCAN COLUMN IN DETAIL

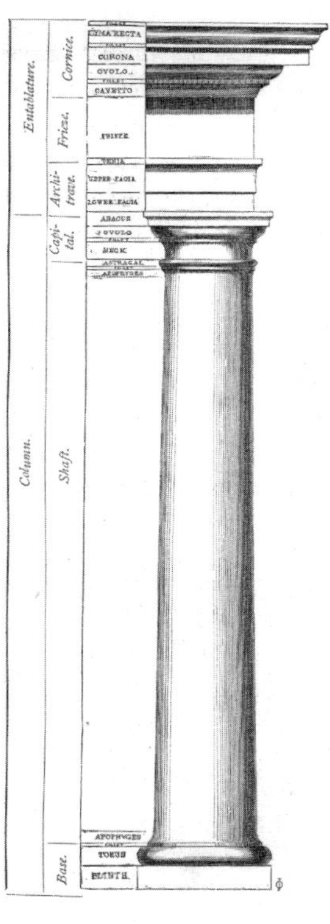

Tuscan, the plainest of the orders, has minimal moulded capitals and a plain entablature above.

This is a variation on the Tuscan order.

DORIC

Doric is the earliest of the Greek orders. It has plain columns, sometimes without a base. The entablature has a row of triple panels called triglyphs.

IONIC

Ionic columns have capitals with a spiral design.

COMPOSITE

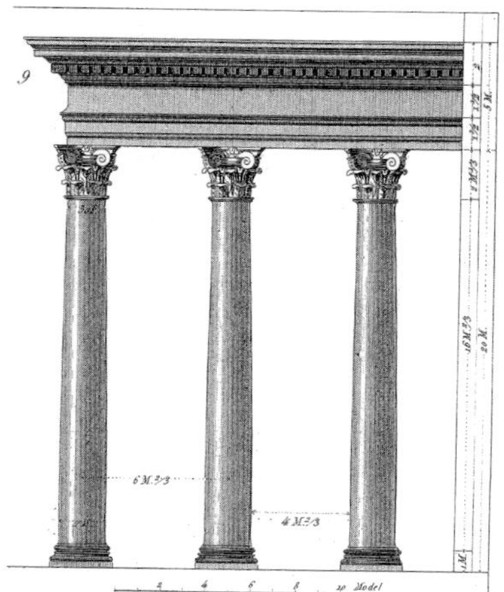

Composite capitals combine the acanthus leaves of the Corinthian order with the spiral design of the Ionic.

CORINTHIAN

The Corinthian order has ornate capitals featuring carved acanthus leaves.

Appendix Two

Development in Architecture: Norman to Gothic

Piers and capitals

NORMAN

The Normans developed a wide range of capital styles, many of which have curved or spiral elements. Some have realistic animal carvings.

EARLY ENGLISH GOTHIC

Stylised foliage (known as stiff-leaf) was a favourite motif of Early English carvers.

DECORATED GOTHIC

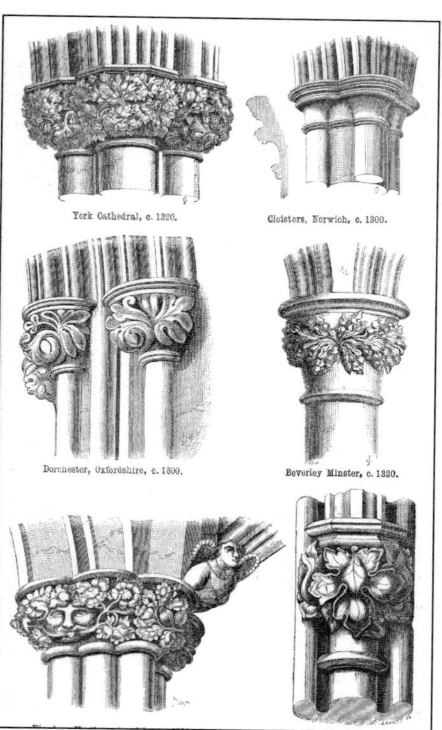

Decorated Gothic capitals can have simple plain mouldings but, in high-status buildings, boast realistic foliage carving.

PERPENDICULAR GOTHIC

Kenton, Devonshire, c. 1500.

Perpendicular capitals can incorporate stylised leaves although, sometimes, they are left very plain.

Windows

NORMAN

Norman windows usually have a single, round-headed opening. There are sometimes mouldings or zigzag ornament around the opening, but often the window is plain.

EARLY ENGLISH GOTHIC

The narrow, pointed lancet is the typical Early English window. Lancets are sometimes grouped symmetrically and flanked with slender shafts.

DECORATED GOTHIC

Decorated Gothic windows often have elaborate tracery making complex, sometimes flowing, patterns.

PERPENDICULAR GOTHIC

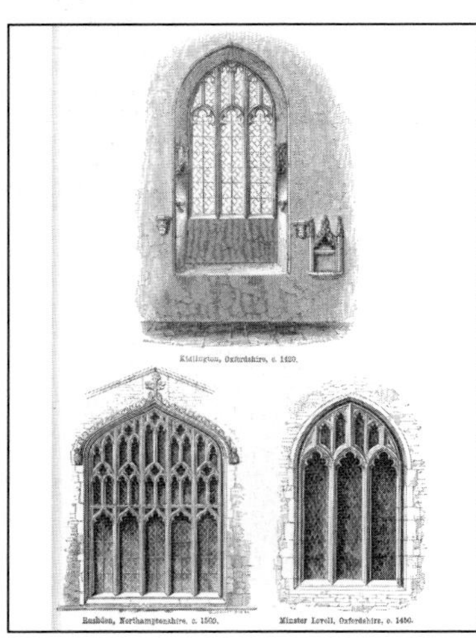

In Perpendicular windows, vertical glazing bars extend right up to the top of the window opening, so the effect is much more linear than in the other kinds of Gothic.

Doorways

NORMAN

In some Norman examples, the zigzag ornament goes up the sides of the doorway as well as around the top.

EARLY ENGLISH GOTHIC

Faringdon, Berkshire, c. 1200. St. Cross, Hampshire, c. 1220.

Uffington, Berkshire, c. 1220. Great Milton, Oxfordshire, c. 1240.

The pointed opening comes in with the dawn of Gothic in the Thirteenth Century.

DECORATED GOTHIC

Doorways, Kislingbury, Northants, c. 1320.

North Mimms, Hertfordshire, c. 1360.

Floral ornaments and multiple mouldings characterise Decorated Gothic doorways.

PERPENDICULAR GOTHIC

Kenton, Devonshire, c. 1500.

Christ Church Hall Staircase, A.D. 1523.

In Perpendicular architecture, doorway openings often have the flattened or four-centred arch with a square moulding above.

Arches

NORMAN

Norman arches are semicircular, sometimes moulded and sometimes very plain. At the end of the period, slightly pointed (transitional) arches appear.

EARLY ENGLISH GOTHIC

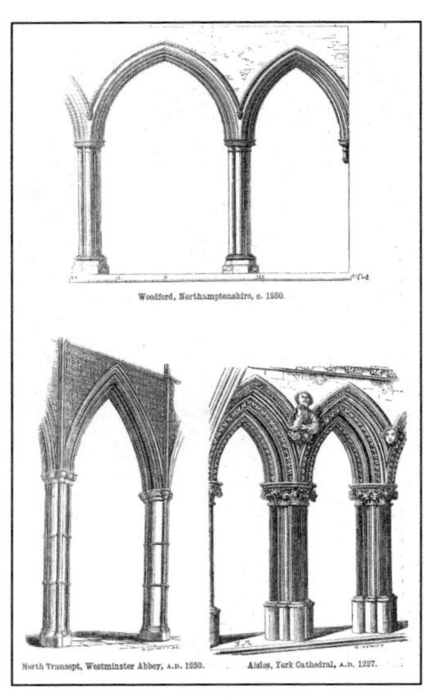

With the dawn of Gothic architecture, piers tend to become more slender and moulded arches are sometimes ornamented with dogtooth and other patterns.

DECORATED GOTHIC

Decorated arches are similar to Early English, but in high-status buildings they can be even more ornate.

PERPENDICULAR GOTHIC

The Perpendicular style displays less carved ornament and more reliance on the continuous lines of shafts and mouldings.

Vaults and roofs

NORMAN

Norman buildings often have quite steeply pitched roofs, although the timbers have usually been renewed. Grander buildings have stone barrel vaults.

EARLY ENGLISH GOTHIC

The typical Early English vault is a simple pointed ribbed vault. Roofs are steeply pitched like the Norman example.

DECORATED GOTHIC

Decorated Gothic roofs vary in design, but can be quite low-pitched. If there is a vault, it has a complex pattern of ribs.

PERPENDICULAR GOTHIC

Perpendicular Gothic roofs are usually low-pitched. In larger buildings there are sometimes fan vaults. Wooden roofs often have an angel in flight, as in this example.

Spires and Pinnacles

NORMAN

Norman spires, where they occur, are simple and plain; the period's pinnacles are like elongated pyramids.

EARLY ENGLISH GOTHIC

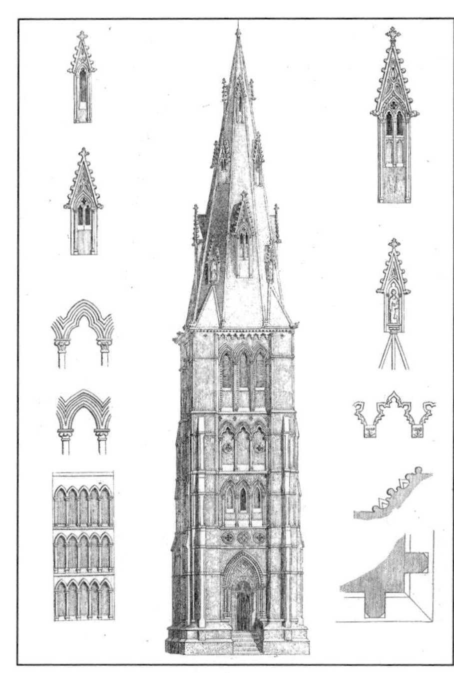

Early Gothic masons developed the broach spire, in which there are small, wedge-shaped supports at the corners of the base.

DECORATED GOTHIC

The typical Decorated spire is ornate, with pinnacles around the base; the pinnacles themselves can be decorated with little protrusions called crockets.

PERPENDICULAR GOTHIC

The Perpendicular period was the heyday of magnificent towers topped with tall, pointed pinnacles at the corners.

This selection of English cathedrals shows the range of effects possible in Gothic architecture, especially the huge variety of shapes of tower and spire.

Picture Sources

The following sources were used for the images in this book:

Campbell, Colen: *Vitruvius Britannicus* (First published, 1715).

Eastlake, C. L.: *A History of the Gothic Revival in England* (Longmans, Green & Co, London, 1872).

Rev Purey-Cust, A. P.: *Our English Minsters* (Isbister & Company, London, c. 1897).

Rickman, Thomas: *Gothia Architectura: An Attempt to Discriminate the Styles of Architecture in England from the Conquest to the Reformation* (Parker & Co, Oxford, 1894).

Spence, H. D. M., the Dean of Gloucester: *The Church of England: A History for the People* in four volumes (Cassell & Company Ltd, 1898).

Postcards courtesy of The Estate of Stanley Shoop.

Images by Nash of Brighton Pavilion courtesy of The Royal Pavilion, Library and Museums, Brighton and Hove.

Index

Numbers in **bold** refer to illustrations